Routledge Introduction

Series Editors:
John Bale and David Drakakis-Smith

The Third World City

In the same series

David Drakakis-Smith

The Third World City

London and New York

First published in 1987 by
Methuen & Co. Ltd

Reprinted 1990, 1992, 1995
by Routledge
11 New Fetter Lane, London EC4P 4EE
29 West 35th Street, New York, NY 10001

© 1987 David Drakakis-Smith

Typeset by Hope Services
Printed in Great Britain
by Clays Ltd, St Ives plc

British Library Cataloguing in Publication Data
Drakakis-Smith, D. W.
The Third World City.—(Routledge introductions to development)
1. Urbanization—Developing countries
I. Title
307.7'64'091724 HT149.5

Library of Congress Cataloguing in Publication Data
Drakakis-Smith, D. W.
The Third World City.
(Routledge introductions to development)
Includes index.
1. Urbanization—Developing countries. 2. Cities and towns—Developing
countries. 3. Urban policy—Developing countries. I. Title. II. Series.
HT169.5.D69   1987   307.7'6'091724   86-21824

ISBN 0-415-05895-3

Contents

Acknowledgements

The author wishes to thank Pauline Jones and May Bowers for typing the manuscript, Muriel Patrick for cartographic work and Don Morriss for photographic work. In addition, he wishes to thank Croom Helm for permission to reproduce figures 1.1, 1.3, 2.2, 2.3, A1, 6.2, H1, H2, I1, I2.

1
Urban growth in the Third World: a global perspective

Introduction

Although most people in the Third World still live in rural areas, the focus for much of the change which has occurred during the colonial and especially the post-colonial periods has been the city. Development strategists from all shades of the political spectrum agree in this respect, although they differ considerably in their assessment of the consequent benefits of such change. It is one of the principal objectives of this book to examine the character of the urbanization process in the Third World and draw some conclusions about the nature of the change it has encouraged.

Urbanization, and more particularly the urbanization process, thus refers to much more than simple population growth and involves an analysis of the related economic, social and political transformations. However, the dimensions of urban population growth do form an essential background to the distribution and extent of the urbanization process, and it is to this topic that this initial chapter now turns. Almost all of the major texts on urbanization contain detailed examinations of these trends, but the most readily comprehensive data are those compiled by the World Bank in its annual World Development Reports.

Questions of definition

It must be admitted at the outset that there is little homogeneity in the nature of urban growth in the Third World, and this is perhaps not surprising in view of the large number and varied nature of the countries involved. Capital cities can range from small agglomerations of less than 20,000 people in the Pacific to the massive 16 million of Mexico City, whilst their growth rates have oscillated between those in excess of 15 per cent per annum (in Papua New Guinea during the 1970s) to actual decline in war-ravaged countries such as Kampuchea.

This diversity also extends to definitions of what is 'urban' or what constitutes a 'city'. In an effort to overcome such variations the United Nations has standardized its data to recognize settlements of over 20,000 people as 'urban', of more than 100,000 as 'cities' and of more than 5 million as 'big cities'.

Although this may seem neat and sensible, it does not overcome the problem of how to define an urban agglomeration or settlement on the ground – to what extent should spatially separate suburbs or individual dwellings be incorporated. The nature of the problem has recently been demonstrated by Richard Kirby in his book *Urbanisation in China* in which he discusses the extent to which Chinese cities often 'annex' a considerable number of adjacent districts into their administrative areas in order to ensure control of vital urban supply needs, such as reservoirs or power plants. As a result many Chinese cities incorporate large rural areas, the populations of which live many miles from the city yet inflate its official population. Llasa, for example, the ancient capital of Tibet, extends over 650 km from east to west, whilst Shanghai's true urban population is nearer to 6 million than the oft cited 12 million.

Moreover, these standardized United Nations definitions are often abandoned in global tabulations where each country's own estimates and proportions are accepted in the production of international comparative statistics, such as those regularly compiled by the World Bank and used in the construction of the maps and graphs in this chapter. Perhaps we should be less insistent on standardized definitions and simply accept what each country considers ought to be its own definition. If this reflects what is historically, culturally and politically 'urban' in that country, then so be it. Why should some arbitrarily acceptable figure be artificially imposed?

Levels of urban population growth

Figure 1.1 reveals very clearly that there are considerably higher levels of urban population as a proportion of national totals in the more developed countries of Europe and North America than in those of the Third World. In very general terms three-quarters of the population in developed countries are urban compared to only one quarter in developing countries.

These broad figures conceal considerable variation within the Third

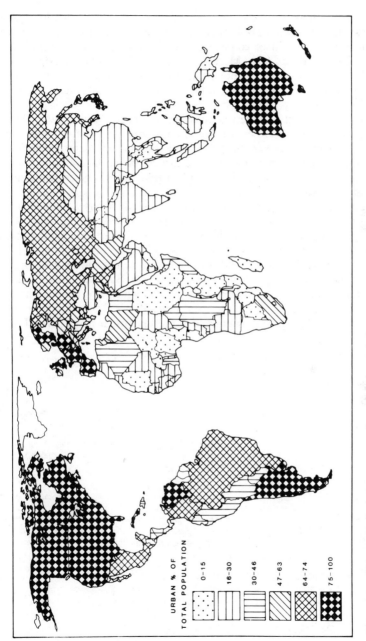

URBAN % OF
TOTAL POPULATION

- 0 – 15
- 16 – 30
- 30 – 46
- 47 – 63
- 64 – 74
- 75 – 100

Figure 1.1 Urban population as a proportion of total population
Source: World Bank (1985) *World Development Report*, Washington DC.

World as a whole, even if simple regional variations are taken into account. For example, many parts of Latin America are as urbanized as Europe, with the urban proportion of countries such as Venezuela and Argentina, in particular, being very high. Moreover, individual cities such as Mexico City and São Paulo are already amongst the most populous in the world and are each predicted to swell to populations well in excess of 20 million by the end of the century.

In contrast, most of Africa is much less urbanized, with some countries having less than 10 per cent of their population concentrated in this way. However, substantial variations from this generalized picture exist in the southern and northern regions where, particularly in the countries fringing the Mediterranean, a much longer urban tradition has given rise to more intensive growth.

Asia appears to be more uniform but its regionally averaged urban proportion of 25 per cent is kept to this level by the arithmetical bias of the huge populations of China, India and Indonesia which are only beginning their period of rapid urban growth. Elsewhere, in the smaller industrializing nations such as Taiwan or South Korea, the percentage living in towns and cities is already nearing half the total population. But the most remarkable feature of the Asian population is the way in which it is characterized by both very large cities and dense rural populations. The contrast between urban and rural life is consequently at its most intense in many parts of Asia.

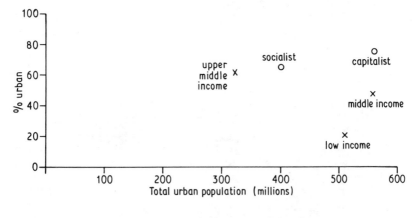

× Developing countries (total urban population = 1405 million)

○ Developed countries (total urban population = 812 million)

Figure 1.2 Urban populations of groups of countries

There are, therefore, considerable variations within and between the various regions and countries of the Third World with respect to the level of urban population. But if the broad contrast with the developed world holds true why should we be so concerned with urban problems in the Third World when people are three times as likely to be urbanized in the west? The answer, of course, lies not in the level of urbanization but in its sheer size and rate of growth.

Rates and scale of growth

In terms of absolute totals the 25 per cent of the Third World resident in towns and cities far exceeds the urban population of the developed countries (figure 1.2). But more crucially the rate of increase of these respective totals is such that the developing world exceeds the developed by a factor of 3 to 1. Figure 1.3, therefore, indicates quite different patterns of urban population growth from figure 1.1 and is more illustrative of countries and regions where rapid urbanization poses severe problems.

To put the comparison into an historical perspective, the urban growth in Europe (including Russia) throughout the whole of the nineteenth century amounted to some 45 million people, a total exceeded by Brazil alone in just the third quarter of the present century. Indeed, between 1950 and 1975 the total urban population of the Third World grew by 400 million and by AD 2000 will have increased by a further 1000 million.

One apparently undeniable feature consequent on this unprecedented scale of growth has been the way in which the largest cities appear to be growing at the most rapid rates. This has given rise to the concept of urban primacy, which is the demographic, economic, social and political dominance of one city over all others within an urban system.

It is undoubtedly true that by AD 2000 the world's twenty most populous cities will have switched from a Euro-American concentration to a clear bias towards the Third World (figure 1.4). It is also true that in some developing countries urban primacy is very marked. In Thailand, for example, Bangkok is nearly fifty times the size of the second city in the country, and contains almost three-quarters of the country's urban population. However, urban primacy is not exclusive to developing countries; it has been and continues to be a feature of many European countries such as Greece, Ireland, Austria and Norway (figure 1.4).

In the past, the preoccupation of some geographers with the urban primacy of the Third World led to the development of theories allegedly illustrative of the way in which this imbalance was reflected in the whole urban system of many countries. These countries were said to be 'over-urbanized' or possessed of 'abnormal' urban hierarchies very different from the predictions of the rank–size rule used in analyses of European and

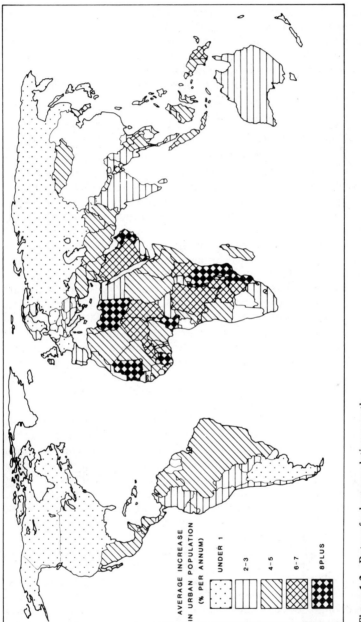

**AVERAGE INCREASE
IN URBAN POPULATION
(% PER ANNUM)**

UNDER 1

2 – 3

4 – 5

6 – 7

8 PLUS

Figure 1.3 Rates of urban population growth
Source: World Bank (1985) World Development Report, Washington D.C.

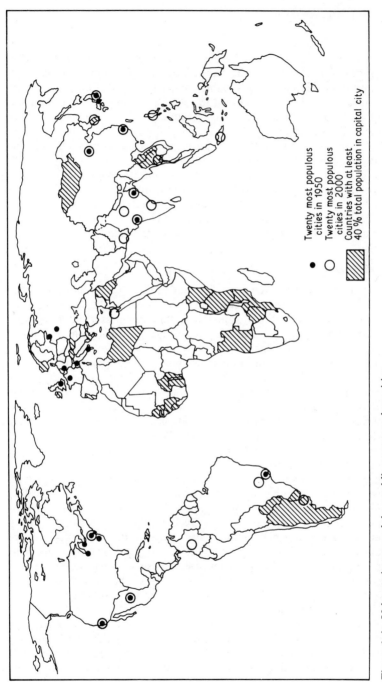

Figure 1.4 Urban primacy and the world's most populous cities

Twenty most populous
cities in 1950

Twenty most populous
cities in 2000

Countries with at least
40% total population in capital city

American urban networks. However, herein lay the weakness of such allegations – they were heavily Eurocentric and formulated on concepts based on unjustified and unjustifiable comparisons with European 'norms' (that have themselves been subject to severe criticism too). Is there really an optimal size of city against which Asian or African settlements may be judged to be abnormal?

This is not to minimize the real problems that rapid urban growth has posed for many Third World cities but it does indicate that they must be assessed in their own regional and national contexts rather than measured against an inappropriate and often mythical European or North American standard or concept. Nothing illustrates more clearly the need to understand the local context and process of urbanization before the problems posed to geographers and urban planners can be fully appreciated.

Urban growth and economic development

In the past many of the attempts to 'explain' rapid urban growth have relied heavily upon the apparently clear-cut links between the level of Gross National Product (GNP) per capita and the urban proportion of total population. As figure 1.5 indicates, these two phenomena have a direct graphical correlation which is all too often interpreted as a causal relationship between urbanization and economic development. But nothing could be further from the truth because GNP per capita is an indicator of economic *growth* rather than *development* (growth with equity), and urban population *levels* do not reflect the complexity of the urbanization *process*. Moreover, which way does the causal relationship operate? Does economic growth follow or precede urban growth? The graph gives no indication of such influences, which will vary from city to city, and simply indicates that a general relationship exists.

Once again, therefore, aggregated data are shown to be rather ambiguous, deficient in representativ e value and devoid of explanatory function. This can be emphasized by comparing figure 1.5 with figure 1.6 which graphs rates of urban and economic growth. Such a graph still lacks explanatory power but, as the previous sections have indicated, its data comprise more useful indicators of urban pressures in the Third World. Thus it is very clear from the graph that an inverse relationship exists between the two sets of statistics and that some of the most rapid urban growth is occurring in the poorest countries – those least able to cope with the resultant pressure on jobs, services and the like.

This pessimistic picture poses the question of why urban population growth should be so high in countries that offer so little in their cities. The reason is, of course, that prospects are even worse in the countryside and it is the perceived advantages of the city that draw migrants to it. However,

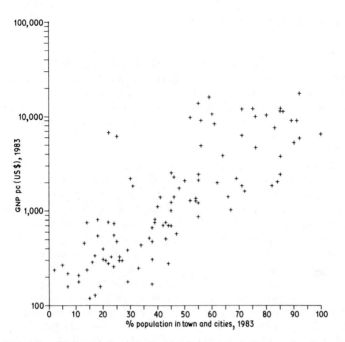

Figure 1.5 The relationship between levels of economic and urban development

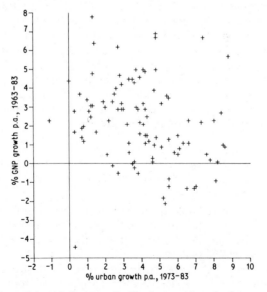

Figure 1.6 The relationship between levels of economic and urban growth

we must not oversimplify the process of rural–urban migration which is a complex and changing phenomenon that is dealt with in more detail in chapter 3 of this book and in Hugo's book in this series, *Population and Development in the Third World*.

Conclusion

What this overview has indicated more than anything else is the diverse nature of global and Third World urbanization. In particular, it is clear that models used to formalize, represent and analyse the past, present and future urban growth patterns of Europe and North America have little relevance for the examination of Third World cities. Not only are their functions and structure quite different, but they exist within a different part of the world economic system. This means that the ability of planners and administrators to respond to urban problems is severely constrained.

All of this is not to deny that much of the urban change which has occurred in the Third World over the last two decades has drawn it closer to the forces that shape western cities. The adoption of western styles of building design, urban planning and consumption values have, therefore, begun to produce a truly global style of capital city in which central business districts are dominated by the same skyscrapers, inhabited by the same international banks, whose employees wear similar clothes and grab Big Macs or Kentucky Fried Chicken for lunch. In this respect Kuala Lumpur and Suva are little different from Rome or Los Angeles. However, the incorporation of Third World nations and cities into the world system, whether capitalist or socialist, is also historically specific and is strongly influenced by local forces and circumstances. This crucial factor must be borne in mind as we try to tease from the complexities of the real world some of the common denominators in this process. In this context there is no better or more appropriate place to start than the historical background to contemporary urbanization in the Third World.

Key ideas

1 Problems exist in defining what is 'urban' and in distinguishing between urban growth and urbanization.
2 Considerable spatial variations exist in the urban proportion of total population within and between developed and developing countries.
3 The level and rate of urban growth are different concepts and do not show similar global patterns.
4 A western bias has characterized past analyses of urban growth and over-simplified economic explanations have been put forward to explain urban growth.

2
The historical perspective: the changing nature of colonial and post-colonial urbanization

Definitions and framework of analysis

The terms 'colonial' and 'imperial' tend to be used interchangeably and indiscriminately in descriptions of pre-independent development. Rather than become involved in what can become a tortuous and tedious debate, this chapter will use a simple and straightforward definition of capitalist colonialism as 'the assumption of political power for economic purposes'. Imperialism will be regarded as encompassing a similar process but within a more formal political framework and in circumstances of more extensive settlement by representatives of metropolitan or colonial power.

Such expatriate settlement could be found in a wide range of circumstances, not only in the large ports we often regard as archetypal of the colonial period, but also in smaller more functionally specialized settlements, such as military garrisons, hill stations or railway towns. Expatriates could also be found in extensive agricultural settlement in areas such as Australia, Dutch East Indies or French North Africa.

Such variation implies that colonial settlement is perhaps not as stereotypical as is often assumed. Indeed, colonialism itself varied enormously across the world according to a complex mix of the particular countries involved and the specific motivation for colonial expansion at the time it occurred. It would be wrong to assume, for example, that pre-colonial Asia and Africa comprised a blank slate of backward, traditional societies on which a common pattern of colonialism was to be inscribed. Some areas did consist of subsistence communities but many others contained nations that were much larger and more sophisticated than the small European countries which were beginning to range overseas for trading commodities.

Nor were these European powers themselves of a uniform character. Although commonly seeking economic profit, their method of exploration, exploitation and administration varied according to cultural characteristics (the British preferred indirect rule through advisors, the French direct incorporation into a centralized metropolitan system) and to the agents and organizations involved – many individuals sought simple plunder, companies sought trading materials, national governments sought spheres of influence.

Above all, this complex spatial intermixture of colonial and pre-colonial influences varied enormously through time. The scramble for territories that we regard as typical of colonialism was, in fact, representative of only a relatively short period of the colonial process. It might, therefore, be helpful to organize this chapter within a simplified framework of these changes. Table 2.1 illustrates the structural evolution of colonialism and will be used not only to describe the characteristics of each phase but also to

Table 2.1   Stages of colonial urbanization in Asia

Chronological phases	Major features of urbanization
Pre-contact	Small, organically patterned towns predominate
1500	
Mercantile colonialism	Limited colonial presence in existing ports. Trade usually in natural products of local region.
1800	
Transitional phase	Reduced European interest in investment overseas. Greater profits to be made in industrial revolution.
1850	
Industrial colonialism	European need for cheap raw materials and food. Colonialism takes territorial form, new settlement patterns and morphology created.
1920	
Late colonialism	Intensification of European morphological influence. Extension to smaller towns in hierarchy. Increased ethnic segregation.
1950	
Early independence	Rapid growth of indigenous populations through migration in search of jobs. Expansion of slum and squatter settlements.
1970	
New International Division of Labour	Appearance of multinational corporation factories. Further migrational growth. Rise of aided self-help programmes.

examine the impact these had upon the colonial city, which is the focus of our particular interest. Note, in particular, that the model relates primarily to Asia in terms of the illustrative time scale. However, although Africa and Latin America differ in this respect, the succession of phases still holds true.

Mercantile colonialism

Initial forays from Europe were made by individual adventurers to obtain inherently valuable objects such as gold and silver. Subsequently the search shifted to commodities that were valued within the European trading system, such as spices, silks or sugar. Often these were obtained not by trade but by simple plunder, although by and large the commodities drawn into the European system were the natural products of their country of origin. This was important because their local collection was left in the hands of existing traders whose networks remained intact and were simply incorporated into the new European markets.

Overall, therefore, there was little need for an extensive European presence on foreign soil, although the nature of mercantile colonialism varied enormously due to the wide range of countries involved and the lengthy period it lasted. In Latin America the earliest contacts were almost entirely destructive of indigenous population and property – whole cities in the Aztec and Inca empires. Elsewhere, particularly in South-east Asia, contact was based on the trade of valuable commodities, often of Chinese origin since no direct European contact was permitted with that empire. The limited European settlement was not only due to efficient local trading networks but also to the fact that mercantile colonialism was based on private company rather than state enterprises. Permanent company representatives were relatively few in number and tended to be confined to spatially limited concession areas within existing indigenous cities.

This situation did not remain static, however, and as profits expanded, so the Europeans began to seek a more extensive presence in order to oversee the collection of the traded commodities. Eventually these warehouses would be protected with troops, first indigenous and later European, whose military technology was such as to ensure superiority despite inferior numbers. Later on, the demand for commodities of reliable quality led to the gradual incursion of European companies into the production process itself, extending their influence well outside the trading concession.

In morphological terms, however, Europeans were usually confined to very small areas of the cities in which they resided. Most of these cities were already organized into ethnic/occupational quarters prior to the European arrival so that one more group made relatively little difference. For example, when the Portuguese assumed control over Malacca in 1511 this merely resulted in a bishop replacing the imam, a governor superseding the sultan, and a fort and church being constructed above the town. Trading in the port continued uninterrupted in the distinct Chinese, Japanese, Arab and Indian quarters. In other cities, where only concessionary rights were obtained, the European impact was even less marked.

There was little planning of the European areas in the contemporary sense of the word. In the early years most Europeans sought simply to reproduce familiar urban forms; for example, the Dutch in Batavia (Java) constructed tall, closely packed houses along its canals, as in the Netherlands. But diseases resultant from the malarial water and the lack of fresh air soon forced an adaptation of the long, low villas of the Javanese aristocracy. Similar trends elsewhere produced a distinctive series of colonial vernacular architectural styles that were European in function and facilities but indigenous in design and materials. In broader terms, the mercantile colonial period had little impact on systems of cities; no new hierarchies were created (unlike later periods) and only in Latin America did settlements of purely colonial origin, such as Buenos Aires and Lima, appear.

By the end of the eighteenth century, European interest in overseas ventures began to moderate, for several reasons, and a transitional period in the nature of colonial development emerges. First, the extensive European wars of the Napoleonic period retained within Europe many of the adventurers on whom mercantile exploration depended – these wars also soaked up most of the funds that backed such enterprises. Second, the shift into production *per se* rather than trade began to inflate the cost of colonial activities beyond the capacity of the companies involved. Several of the largest and most famous went into liquidation during this period, such as the Dutch voc which collapsed in 1799, and their operations were taken over by the respective state governments.

But the principal characteristic of the transitional period was the interest of European investors in the greater profits to be made from the industrial revolution rather than mercantile colonialism. In this context it is not surprising that Francis Light, Stamford Raffles and Charles Elliot found the British government less than enthusiastic about the development of their 'acquisition' of Penang, Singapore and Hong Kong respectively. Palmerston's famous dismissal of Hong Kong as 'a barren island with hardly a house upon it' encapsulated the feeling of the investors, both private and public, of the period.

Industrial colonialism

Such sentiments did not persist for very long. The rapid growth of the European industrial revolution led to increasing demands for both raw materials and food for the burgeoning urban work-force. By the third quarter of the nineteenth century European capital was once again being invested overseas but on this occasion the principal agent of organization was the state. The accumulation of raw materials and food required more than trading toe-holds; it depended on the acquisition of territory and the organization of production in order to keep costs as low as possible. Much of the food was produced in colonies where European settlement was more extensive. In the British case this was Australia, Canada and South Africa. Elsewhere, physical constraints restricted European settlement to the management and administration of raw material production. Often this was no longer of indigenous crops but of introduced commodities, such as rubber in Malaysia, which required the wholesale restructuring of society, even to massive importation of foreign labour.

As might be imagined, all of this had a far reaching impact on urbanization in the new colonies, but there have been relatively few attempts to rationalize what happened in terms of a general theory that encompasses the industrial colonial period as a whole. Of these by far the most useful is that by Anthony King in his book *Colonial Urban Development* (see further reading list).

King suggests that the economic motivation within colonialism was translated into spatial form through three main intermediary forces:

Culture

The cultural values of any society, whether social, legal or religious, give rise to a set of institutions which determine much of the physical form of that culture. The various cultural elements of Victorian British society were therefore reflected in the built form of its colonial settlements: churches, theatres, men's clubs. This would also extend to the conventional standards acceptable for middle-class housing, a factor which is linked to the second intermediary force translating colonialism into physical form, that is technology.

Technology

The principal contrast between metropolitan and colonized societies in this respect was the extensive use of inanimate sources of energy, compared to animal and human portage. In terms of transportation this led to the introduction of railways and broad boulevards which devastated the old, medieval street patterns of many existing cities. But the impact was greater than this direct repercussion because European society had already made major spatial adjustments to its own technology, namely the separation of workplace and residence, and the emergence of functionally specialized buildings. New social organizations were also needed to cope with this complex urban system – police forces, transport companies, construction firms and the like. Little wonder that existing urban morphologies were abandoned in favour of new urban districts in which the European

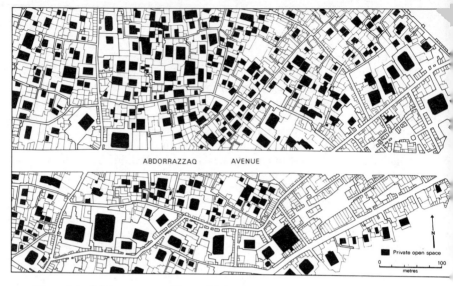

Figure 2.1 Isfahan: new road in an old city

Plate 2.1 Kuala Lumpur railway station showing the hybrid British-Moslem architecture of this pinnacle of colonial technology

technology could be incorporated (figure 2.1). Such districts were characterized by wide, straight roads and specialized land uses and are almost inevitably focused on the pinnacle of nineteenth-century technological achievement – the railway station – the architectural personification of industrial colonialism (plate 2.1).

Political structure

The factor which enabled the wholesale introduction of new technological and cultural values was the political control exercised by the Europeans. Nineteenth-century colonial society consisted of a two-tier dominant–subordinate relationship of colonizers and colonized and it is important to appreciate that its cities were organized around the control of the economy rather than around the production process itself. There was only limited manufacturing in nineteenth-century colonial cities: production was usually confined to rural agriculture or concentrated mining locations. The occupational structure within the cities therefore reflected this political and economic relationship, with a small, metropolitan administrative élite and a large supportive population engaged in the tertiary sector, the production and distribution of consumer goods and services. As the colonial élite also controlled the municipal government, the city could be shaped according to the wishes of a small proportion of its total residents.

Urban development in the industrial colonial period

Colonial influence upon urban systems was, in contrast to the mercantile period, felt at all levels within the urban hierarchy, although variations existed according to time and location. In some areas it is claimed that entirely new urban hierarchies were created – in Malaya for example. In others, such as North Africa, there was wholesale reorientation of urban economic activity from inland trading routes to the new coastal entrepôts.

Much of the reorientation was due to the revalued spatial priorities of the new colonialism and was highly selective in its impact. It is this period, therefore, that sees the genesis of contemporary urban primacy as economic and political power is concentrated on certain cities at the expense of others. In settler colonies, such as Zimbabwe, this led to urban development being limited to white regions of the country – a pattern that has persisted through to the present (figure 2.2).

Within the colonial cities too, similar patterns of social, economic and spatial segregation were being reinforced. Although manufacturing was limited, a large commercial and service sector existed to meet the trading and consumer needs of the colonial power. Much of this activity was functionally specific to ethnic and class groups within the city. The foreign component of the trading system was dominated by Europeans and their

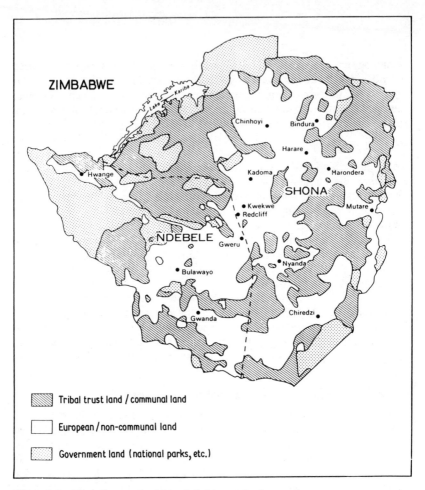

Figure 2.2 Zimbabwe: colonial land division and urban settlement

institutions, the famous trading firms such as Jardine Matheson in the Far
East. Local assembly and distribution of the goods involved was in the hands
of expatriate non-Europeans; only local production, under expatriate
supervision, was the function of indigenous populations. In this system the
expatriate non-Europeans played a crucial role. Often imported specifically
for this role, the Chinese and Indians in South-east Asia and tropical Africa
constituted an economic, social and political buffer between the Europeans
and the indigenous masses. The face-to-face haggle over commodities in the
market-place thus occurred between non-European groups and redirected
ethnic conflict and antagonism away from the dominant colonial minority.

This functional distinction was reinforced by ethnic spatial separation with the cities. Although this separation had long been practised before the coming of Europeans, the new colonial planners refined and accentuated it by astute use of town-planning regulations. Many of the health and building regulations were enforced only in the European districts which were effectively separated from non-European zones by the cordon sanitaire of open spaces provided by parks, race-courses and railway lines, reinforced by judiciously placed military cantonments (see case study A, below). The remarkable feature of the urban morphologies of colonial cities from large to small was the way in which they were almost totally dominated by the *lebensraum* of what usually remained a demographic minority.

Case study A

Delhi: the evolution of an imperial city

The pre-colonial city

When the British arrived in Delhi the city was still the Mogul capital of North India, although it was in the hands of rebels and its population had fallen to about 150,000. Almost all lived within the city wall which was 9 km long and enclosed an area of about 6.5 km^2. At the heart of the city were the political, religious and commercial foci of the Royal Palace, the Jama Mosque and Chadni Chowk respectively (figure A.1). The remainder comprised an organically patterned pre-industrial city of narrow, twisting lanes and mixed land uses – not dissimilar to those of medieval Europe.

The period of coexistence 1803–57

In its early colonial years Delhi was not a major administrative or commercial centre, merely a district military post for the Punjab. There were no more than a few hundred Europeans and, as the situation was very stable, the military cantonment was located to the north-west of the city, with most of the British living in the city itself in an area adjacent to the Royal Palace (where a puppet emperor still reigned) previously occupied by the Mogul aristocracy. Western technology was barely in evidence apart from some institutional architecture, and most of the British lived in the same manner as the indigenous élites. There was little social contact between the races but little conflict either. So, although there was a political dualism, the retention of the court meant that this was not profound and was barely reflected in lifestyle or technology. The principal contrast, therefore, was cultural.

Case study A (*continued*)

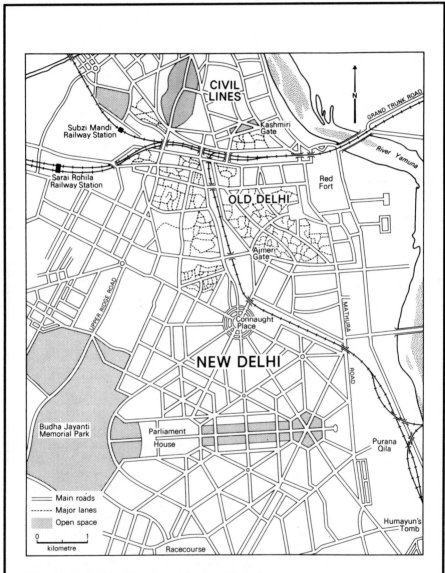

Figure A.1   Delhi: old and new urban morphologies

Case study A (*continued*)

Colonial consolidation 1857–1911

The pressures of nineteenth-century colonial expansion erupted in India in the mutiny of 1857 in which the Mogul emperor was implicated and dethroned. The consequent sharpening of military control resulted in a more forceful imposition of political power and cultural values. The Royal Palace became Delhi Fort and a free-fire zone, 500m wide, was created around it and the city walls. The military cantonment occupied the northern third of the city and civilians were moved out to the civil lines to the north of the walls where several physically imposing buildings were constructed as institutional symbols of power. The indigenous population was thus confined to the remaining area of the old city which, although crowded, was still functionally and socially sound.

Culturally, however, Old Delhi and its population became increasingly isolated as the British withdrew to a distinct area to the north, separated by the military zone, police lines, newly constructed gardens and, above all, by the railways. Poor communications had been blamed for many of the problems of the mutiny, and by 1911 eight separate railways had been linked to the city, further eroding the area available to the indigenous population which had by then reached some 230,000.

Thus the full utilization of political power had, within the space of some fifty years, transformed the appearance of Delhi with cultural contrasts spatially accentuated through the medium of a superior military and transportational technology. By 1911 almost a quarter of a million Indians were crammed into 4 km^2 of the old city, whilst a few thousand British enjoyed the relatively open spaces of the northern districts.

Imperial Delhi 1911–47

The new railway technology enabled Delhi to be chosen as the new centralized capital of a consolidated India – the jewel in George V's imperial crown. It was not until 1921, however, that the physical site was moved southwards to a new location in the crook of the Aravalli Hills. New Delhi was planned on a vast scale; as early as 1931 it covered 78 km^2. This was due to the incorporation of new technological developments, the motor car and the telephone, which in theory enabled such large distances to be bridged. In fact, such technology spread only slowly and erratically and for many years communications depended on people power.

There was no provision for manufacturing growth in the new capital, although the city had acquired several important processing industries such

Plate A.1   Old Delhi: View from the Jama Mosque of the intensive development of Old Delhi as a consequence of segregationalist colonial city planning

as flour milling. But the most extraordinary example of colonial influence in urban planning was the minute residential stratification of New Delhi into rigid spatial categories based on the infinitely complex combination of Indian, British, military, civil and colonial ranking systems. This resulted in several designated zones (figure A.1) within which occurred futher stratification of size of house, garden and facing direction in relation to the social Mecca of Government House.

The old city received some improvements to drainage and water supply systems but, as in most colonial cities, urban planning was primarily reserved for the expatriate zones. Old Delhi became even more physically and socially isolated by more gardens and a spacious new business district. As a result in-migration led to massive overcrowding, deterioration of the urban fabric and overspill into rapidly growing squatter areas to the west and east of the old city (plate A.1). Not surprisingly, by the Second World War death rates in Old Delhi were five times those in the new capital.

Independence did not change this contrast very much. Ten years after this event Old Delhi still contained 60 per cent of the city's population at an average density of 41,300 per km^2. But even this was but a foretaste of what was to come later as the capital's population quadrupled to its present size of almost 6 million.

Late colonialism

The inter-war years are in general a poorly investigated period in colonial urban development. In part this is due to the Europeans' renewed preoccupation with their own affairs – two horrendous wars and an intervening economic recession. The latter resulted in erratic demand for the primary products of the colonies and profits became unreliable. In some areas this resulted in the introduction of efficiencies through economies of scale and smaller producers began to be ousted by land reforms and mechanization.

This began to accelerate the drift of rural labour to the towns where, to some extent, it was incorporated into an expansion of factory-based production, but as yet this was limited in scale. The growth in indigenous populations appears to have had relatively little impact on urban planning. Although squatter settlements began to appear, the principal morphological change occurred in European quarters where colonial architecture and land-use planning reached their most grandiose form. It was in the late colonial period that the huge institutional legacies of city halls, universities, banks and the like were bequeathed to the contemporary world (plates 2.2 and 2.3). More and more, the cities were becoming increasingly detached from indigenous rural life. One Malaysian writer, Lim Heng Kow, described Kuala Lumpur in the 1930s as 'a city of European government buildings, European and Oriental banks and businesses, and Chinese and Indian traders or workers, with occasional residual patches of the otherwise submerged Malay world'.

Although the late colonial period saw little structural change in the city, there was in certain colonies an important demographic transformation. This was the accelerated migration from the European recession of large numbers of blue- and white-collar workers. British migrants could settle in largely British communities in the dominions of Canada, Australia or New Zealand, but the French, Dutch and Belgians still comprised minority groups, albeit quite extensive, in their colonies in North and Central Africa and South-east Asia.

Increasingly such migrants began to infiltrate lower white-collar or retail occupations not hitherto favoured by Europeans. Even in British Rangoon well over one-quarter of the European population in 1931 could be classified as traders, shop assistants or unskilled/semi-skilled labour. One unforeseen, but eventually momentous, consequence of this expatriate influx was that the slowly expanding group of educated indigenous residents found it difficult to break into middle-income occupations in either commerce or administration. Their subsequent drift to a Europe riven by political extremism quickly transformed many into political activists who eventually played an important role in the independence struggles in their own countries.

Plate 2.2   Georgetown Penang: City Hall ⎱   both examples of grandiose colonial
Plate 2.3   Singapore: Raffles Hotel   ⎰   architecture

Early independence period

The 1950s and 1960s saw independence spread rapidly throughout most of Asia and Africa, although in those areas where the inter-war European settlement had been substantial, such as Algeria or Java, decolonization was often slow and bitterly contested by colonists who had little to gain from returning to a war-ravaged Europe.

Once the colonial powers had departed there was a great surge of indigenous peoples into their cities, attracted by the prospect of jobs in the lucrative administrative and commercial positions from which they had been excluded. However, in the early years of independence such jobs were relatively few, given the persistence of European control within commercial enterprises and the sluggishness of demand for primary materials from a shattered European industrial economy.

Ironically one of the major problems in Europe was shortage of labour – of which the cities in the newly independent Third World had far too much. The result was an encouragement to this 'surplus' labour to move to employment in north-west Europe. Initially the movement was from former colonies to former metropolitan powers, for example Algerians to France, or Indians to Britain, but it soon spread to many other poor countries, particularly those around the Mediterranean Sea.

For European industrialists and governments this migrant labour was an economic lifeline. It was abundant, non-unionized, cheap and docile (being easily threatenable with permit withdrawal), and for two decades the economic miracles of several West European countries were firmly built on the back of this exploited labour. For their part, Third World governments were only too glad to encourage such a move since it helped decelerate urban population growth, increased foreign exchange revenues through savings sent home and, they hoped, trained some of their workforce.

The build-up of workers in Europe was rapid and highly concentrated. By the late 1960s West Germany and France alone had some 6 million guest-workers between them, with particular concentrations in industrial cities and in the 'dirtier' or 'monotonous' types of employment. But for the donor countries there was comparatively little reward. They lost large numbers of their younger and most useful workers; a few migrants received useful skills or training; and the remittance money was mostly used to finance small consumer businesses in the big cities on the return of the migrant – thus accentuating the original problem.

Overall the immediate post-war years saw little change in the economy of most Third World cities. They continued to be dominated by commercial and trading activities which in turn were still in the hands of expatriate firms. It was simply another form of colonialism.

The biggest change was in the emergence of a huge subsector of the urban population who were unable to acquire waged employment and who were excluded by their poverty from acquiring adequate housing, education and health care for themselves and their families. Such households began to look inwards for their survival and create their own economic system in which meagre incomes were earned in a variety of illegal and semi-legal activities and spent within a production system that specialized in the creation of a consumer market apparently operating outside the formal supply network. This has come to be known as the 'informal sector' or 'petty-commodity production' and is examined in more detail in chapter 5.

Neo-colonialism and the New International Division of Labour

In the late 1960s and early 1970s the world economic system began to change drastically with regard to its incorporation of Third World labour. In Europe the migrants had become more organized, less docile, less cheap and less welcome to both employers and workers as the global recession began to take effect. Accordingly, many European and North American companies began to shift their points of production into the cities of the Third World where cheap labour still existed and could be guaranteed by authoritarian governments reliant on the west for political support. This shift, which is still going on, has come to be known as the New International Division of Labour – NIDL for short – and it is worthwhile finishing off this chapter by outlining some of its main features and impact on contemporary cities in developing countries.

It is perhaps worth noting at the outset that NIDL is not in fact new. Throughout the colonial periods there had always been a contrast between the colonies and the metropolitan power, with the latter undertaking most of the manufacturing production. The main reason why this production has now shifted to Third World cities is because of the rise of what is known as finance capital. This comprises investment funds that have been accumulated by organizations concerned with the management of money – big banks, insurance firms and the like.

Over the last decade these investment funds have increasingly gone to enterprises with Third World factories – not directly into Third World factories, but to multinational corporations, such as Cadbury-Schweppes or Lonrho, who are operating or willing to operate in developing countries. Why should this have occurred?

In the first place, as we have seen, the costs of production have risen in Europe – not only for wages but for rents and raw material imports too. Second, labour is cheap in Third World cities as a result of accelerating rural–urban migration (itself the consequence of capitalist penetration of the countryside – see Chris Dixon's book on agricultural systems and rural development in this series). Third, the presence of the large informal sector, a reserve army of labour, helps keep down the demand for wage rises. Fourth, the recent advances in technology have enabled fragmentation of the production process from management. The advent of computers, telex, satellite links and containerization has meant that it is possible for the labour-intensive parts of the production process to be located in Third World cities, whilst retaining specialist management, research and development in the metropolitan country. Finally, this entire process has been encouraged by international agencies and national governments all anxious to bring employment to the burgeoning cities of the Third World in order to forestall possible political instability.

The impact of these changes on the cities of developing countries has been varied and complex (and will be examined in more detail in chapters 5 and 6). Perhaps the most important thing to notice here is that such changes have been extremely selective, so that some six or seven countries, such as South Korea or Taiwan, can be said to have rapidly expanded their industrial economy. However, as labour costs rise in these locations, so the multinational corporations are looking further afield for new supplies of cheap urban labour. By and large it is the already large cities, with burgeoning populations and infrastructural facilities, that have received the brunt of the investment. This in its turn has induced a third wave of migration into such cities – not all of it being from within the country concerned (see Findlay and Findlay's book in this series).

The social effect has been considerable in the area of class formation. A waged proletariat is now appearing in many cities. Being more privileged than many of their fellow citizens they form a conservative labour group. In contrast, the informal sector has continued to proliferate and many outside observers fear that continued deprivation and frustration may induce a demand for revolutionary change. Moreover, in some countries where new ethnic groups have been attracted into the city, another dimension of urban instability has appeared. A final area of social change has been the unprecedented incorporation of women into the urban work-force, a phenomenon very different from the early years of independence.

All of these changes have been undertaken in most cities with the assistance and co-operation of national governments. The role of the state in taking over the management of capital cities from local authorities has been a crucial step in facilitating the penetration of NIDL. As one might imagine, however, this urban economic transformation has led to unprecedented demands on basic services in Third World cities – demands for housing, transportation and social services that most governments have been unable or unwilling to meet.

Not surprisingly, it is this range of recent economic and social changes and their consequences that form the focus for the remainder of this book on the contemporary Third World city. What this historical chapter has done is to emphasize the fact that we cannot hope to understand their true nature without appreciating the global setting of their evolution.

Key ideas

1   Colonialism was not a uniform process and varied enormously through space and time, and in relation to the cultures involved.
2   The urban impact of mercantile colonialism was very limited.
3   The impact of 'high colonialism' was extensive both on urban hierarchies and on individual city morphologies.
4   Culture, technology and political power transformed economic objectives into urban form.
5   The major changes to this situation did not come with independence but following changes in the world economic system in the 1970s.

3
Demographic aspects of post-colonial urbanization

Introduction

The previous chapters have established that Third World urbanization has undergone tremendous acceleration and change over the last two decades. This chapter will examine the two main components of this population expansion – migration and natural growth – not only to re-emphasize their relative importance (this has been done in chapter 1 and is also discussed in the broader demographic setting by Hugo and by Findlay and Findlay in this series), but also to try to tease out of the discussion some of the forces which have influenced individual families in their decisions on these matters. In this way we can place some of the general economic and political issues raised in the previous chapter into the household context.

The two components of urban population growth vary in relative importance through space and time, but in general migration is more important in the early stages of urban population growth when the proportion of national population living in towns and cities is low (figure 3.1). As the urban population rises, so does the contributary role of natural growth, although only up to a certain point. Beyond this point, which is related more to the demographic cycle than to the absolute size of urban population, urban fertility begins to decline and migrational growth once again becomes more important, albeit at a drastically reduced level.

Migration to the city

It must be noted at the outset that increased economic pressure on the rural household does not always result in urban migration within the country

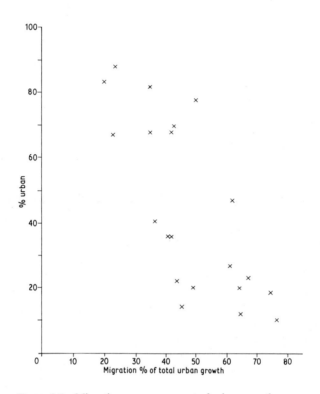

Figure 3.1   Migration as a component of urban growth

concerned. Some governments have successfully deflected migration to other rural areas or, as the previous chapter illustrated, to developed countries. However, by far the most common response is internal migration to towns and cities.

Until recently it has been assumed that the largest settlements have borne the brunt of this migration – assumptions apparently verified by the sheer numbers crowding into capital cities. However, such conclusions have largely been made in the absence of data on medium- and small-sized towns. As this information has been obtained, it has become clear that these settlements have also been affected by migration, perhaps even more dramatically than large cities because they are centres of both in- and out-migration within the urban hierarchy.

Such upheavals are not really reflected in the collated data available on this topic because the double flow of migration tends to balance out, giving

Table 3.1   Average annual rates of growth and city size in developing countries

	1950–60	*1960–70*	*1970–80*	*1980–90*
20,000–99,999	4.9	1.2	0.1	− 0.5
100,000–499,999	4.2	3.5	4.4	2.6
500,000–999,999	3.5	4.1	5.4	4.4
1 million or more	8.2	5.4	5.6	5.6

Source: D. Rondinelli (1982) 'Intermediate cities in developing countries', *Third World Planning Review*, 4(4).

the impression of a stagnant population (table 3.1). One must also be cautious about such data because some capital cities are still relatively small and will appear in the intermediate categories of tables such as table 3.1, although they are the final migrant destination within their country. In addition, as cities grow, they will change categories so that the most rapidly expanding centres will sooner or later work their way into the top rank, taking their growth rates with them. But perhaps the most important criticism is that such tables do not incorporate the 'hidden' urbanization of circular migration in which long-term commuters retain their rural base and are not revealed as migrants in census data.

Explaining urban migration

It is very easy to produce a set of data to indicate the discrepancies in living conditions between rural and urban areas (table 3.2). But averaged figures such as these must be treated with considerable caution. Most migrants will never aspire to, let alone attain, an average urban income – which is usually inflated by a small number of very wealthy people. Similarly, access to many of the more prominent urban facilities, such as hospitals, schools and universities, will be denied to large numbers of the urban poor so that they must be rather suspect incentives to migrate.

However, the few longitudinal migration studies which have been undertaken reveal that the real reasons for movement can change several times during the process itself. In one study in the Calcutta region, successive years of drought were the principal cause for many to leave their small subsistence farms. This was later explained as a move to seek temporary family assistance in nearby towns; later, after the move had become permanent, it was rationalized as a search for improved incomes and a better life-style in the city. The point that needs to be emphasized here is that migration usually occurs initially in response to events (natural, economic, social or political) over which those affected have little control.

Table 3.2   Rural and urban comparisons

	Ratio of GRP* richest/poorest region	Infant mortality per 1000 Urban	Rural
Argentina	9.3		
Brazil	10.0		
China**	4.4		
Columbia	6.8		
India	2.2	60	139
Iran	10.0		
Malaysia	3.6	35	53
Mexico	5.4	79	97
South Korea	2.2		
Thailand	6.3	30	74
Venezuela	6.3		
Yugoslavia	5.7		

Notes: * Gross Regional Product.
     ** regional expenditure per capita.

Migrants and migration

Migration is not an individual affair, even when only one person migrates. Usually it is the consequence of a collective decision involving immediate and extended family members together with any other friends who may be able to provide relevant comment. It is seldom a hasty decision but rather one made on accumulated information on the perceived opportunities available in the city.

Although the decision to move is likely to be a family affair, migrants themselves tend to be self-selective because of their personal attributes. However, the most 'suitable' member of a household may still be uneducated and unprepared for the problems of life in the city and fail to obtain an acceptable income, even within the meagre expectations they have. As time progresses those migrants who have remained in the city are joined by others less able and more dependent, increasing substantially the costs of feeding and housing the migrant household. It is often at this point that migrant households shift from small, rented shelter near the city centre to expanding squatter communities where there is more housing space at lower costs (see chapter 6).

However, even taking such caveats into account, there are usually real differences in income levels after migration. In Delhi, for example, although most casual labourers find work for only eight months of the year, this is double their employment period as rural labourers. Moreover, hourly rates are usually slightly higher in the city. These slight differences are vitally important for poor people, although they say more about the abject poverty of many rural areas than the returns to labour in the city.

The apparently clear-cut nature of such contrasts has willed many economists into producing models aimed largely at predicting migration rates through rural–urban income differences. At its simplest this reduces migration to a straightforward choice between a traditional, backward, rural way of life and a modern, industrialized lifestyle in the city. But this contrast rarely exists in reality in the contemporary Third World. As a result of improved transportation and other communicational developments, particularly the spread of radio, urban values and goods have long since penetrated even the remotest regions; a process which is reinforced by return migration. In parallel, traditional, rural values have moved into the city with the migrants and are retained through the tendency for people of similar backgrounds to cluster together. Indeed, in many ways it is the blurring of distinctions which has served to encourage migration because there is not now such a drastic change of lifestyles involved.

In many instances migration is spatially and historically specific and it is difficult to draw meaningful generalizations of the old 'push-pull' type. Much of the over-simplification is the result of the principal source of information being the migrant who explains the movement after the event has occurred. This is often couched in terms of immediate concerns, usually employment. So migration is rationalized into a movement in search of work.

The physical move itself is heavily dependent on personal contacts, occurring within what anthropologists call a 'spatially extended social field' of kin, tribe or community links which is held together by traditional values related to mutual obligations. Once in the city, it is the same family or friends that usually provide early accommodation and assist in obtaining work.

For many years a stereotypical pattern was assumed to characterize the bulk of migration, i.e. that most migrants were adult males, the vanguard of a later family shift, who sought work in a series of step-like moves up the urban hierarchy at increasing distance from their point of origin. In other words, they would first migrate to a nearby small town, learn some skills and establish an income, then move on to a larger settlement with a greater range of opportunities. Later moves might be by sons or grandsons, with families catching up from time to time.

Such stereotyped movement no longer dominates migration patterns. Much of this is due to new transport developments which have made longer-distance travel easier and cheaper, often at the expense of local destinations. For example, Roi Et, a small town in north-east Thailand, has two buses a week making the 900-km trip to the capital Bangkok – a much better service than to the regional capital of Khon Khaen. As a result many migrants tend to make a direct, long-distance move to a larger city (see case study B, p. 34).

Fiji: migration to the city

The South Pacific islands have been part of the migration process for many years. All are populated by Melanesian or Polynesian peoples who have a long tradition of movement across the Pacific. During the colonial period European powers introduced contract labour from many thousands of miles away to work on plantations.

Fiji is the most populous island nation in the South Pacific, apart from New Zealand. Its current population of some 700,000 is sharply divided along ethnic lines as a result of the British colonial introduction of large numbers of Indian sugar-plantation workers. Many eventually settled in Fiji

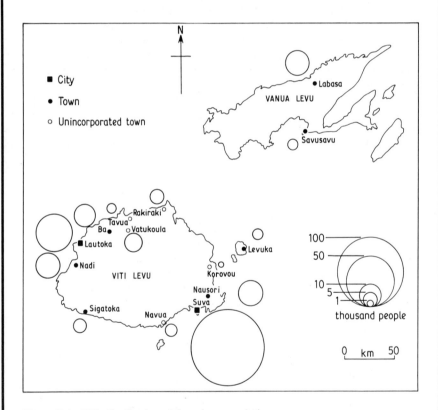

Figure B.1 Fiji: distribution of the urban population
Source: after R.C. Walsh (1977) 'Urbanization in Fiji', *Perspective*, 14

as tenant farmers. At present about 42 per cent of the population is Fijian Melanesian and some 51 per cent is Indian.

As Indians are not allowed to own land in Fiji, it is understandable that many would drift into the towns where they found employment in commerce or industry. After independence in 1970 many Fijians too began to move to the urban areas, drawn by the prospect of administrative jobs.

At present almost 40 per cent of Fiji's population is urbanized and of these half are rural-born. The primary reason for this migration is the opportunity differentials between urban and rural areas. One survey indicated that incomes in the rural provinces were only one quarter of the per capita incomes in Suva, the capital. Moreover, over the last few decades urban incomes have been growing six times as rapidly as rural incomes. There are, however, other reasons for migration; many Fijians, for example, move to the town to escape the traditional social structure, which is based on communalism, in order to accumulate individual wealth.

Urban centres in Fiji are growing at just under 4 per cent per annum, almost double that of the population as a whole. Urban growth has long been dominated by the capital city of Suva and its near neighbour Nausori (figure B.1), which account for some 60 per cent of total urban population

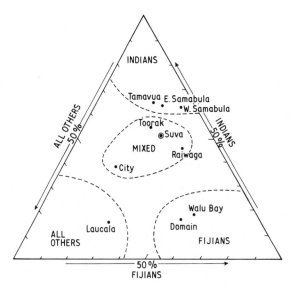

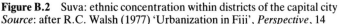

Figure B.2   Suva: ethnic concentration within districts of the capital city
Source: after R.C. Walsh (1977) 'Urbanization in Fiji', *Perspective*, 14

Case study B (*continued*)

and almost one quarter of the national population. As with migrants in most parts of the Third World, cultural and regional ties exercise considerable influence over the direction and destination of the move. There is, therefore, a tendency for certain towns to be favoured by Fijians or Indians, and within the larger centres, such as Suva, there is also concentration within districts (figure B.2).

As with most rapid urban growth in the Third World, the price of this migratory influx has been high. Some rural areas have been seriously depopulated, threatening the livelihood of those who remain. For example, in 1981 only 32 per cent of the people from the island of Rotuma still lived on it, compared to 56 per cent in 1966. Most of the rest were in Suva. In the capital city itself, one of the most serious social problems to emerge in the last ten years has been the housing shortage. As a result of the government's inability to cope, one in nine residents of Suva are squatters (a rise of 16 per cent since 1978) who now comprise a very visible element of the urban townscape (plate B.1).

Plate B.1   Suva, Fiji: squatters on steep hillsides overlooking the port, the main sources of casual employment

In widespread areas of the Third World transport improvements have resulted in circular migration which is really long-term commuting, with the migrant retaining a rural home but moving to the city for weeks or months at a stretch. This is, of course, a common-sense response by the poor who are attempting to obtain the 'best' of both worlds by reducing expensive living costs in the city and retaining rural land revenues or food sources: a process of 'earning in the city, spending in the village'. Many urban employers welcome this trend too, because it keeps wages low since circular migrants often live in very cheap lodgings. The main problems are posed for the urban authorities whose cities are swelled for most of the year by such migrants and who must meet their housing, food, transport and health needs when these arise.

Closely linked to the shift to circular migration has been the other marked change in trends which is the rapid growth of female migration to the city. Some countries have always had comparable levels of female migration, particularly those where rural land holdings are in tenure farms and where there is little economic incentive for the family not to accompany the male migrant. However, over the last ten years there has been a massive upsurge in the demand for female labour in the city following the expansion of factories in the Third World, discussed in the previous chapter.

Much female labour is short-duration and targeted at obtaining a dowry prior to marriage. It is, therefore, non-unionized, docile and very cheap. Women also tend to be more dexterous than men in the intricate assembly industries of the multinational corporations. As a result women now exceed male migrants in the 15-to-25-year age groups, particularly in those countries gaining a reputation for industrial growth (figure 3.2).

Government responses to migration

Many of the responses to migration lie beyond the scope of this particular text and can be found in other books in this series. However, it is worth reviewing the range of options open to Third World governments and drawing some general, if brief, conclusions about their popularity and success, because these have had considerable impact on attitudes towards the second component of urban population growth, natural increase.

It must not be assumed that all governments share a common enthusiasm for curbing migrational growth – after all, urban industrial expansion depends on cheap labour which in turn is linked to continued population growth. However, international agencies are often more concerned with the threat to political stability posed by the continued build-up of urban poor. As Robert McNamara, former President of the World Bank, warned 'if cities do not begin to deal more constructively with poverty, poverty may begin to deal more destructively with cities'. Curbs to rural–urban migration have been seen as part of this programme.

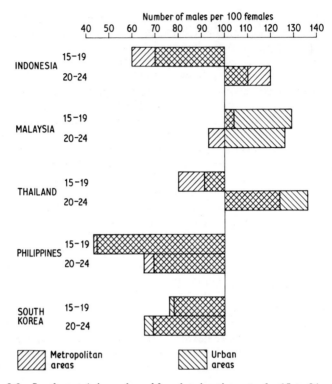

Figure 3.2   South-east Asia: male and female migration rates for 15- to 24-years age groups

Of course, the most appropriate responses to rural out-migration must be those that directly address poverty and underdevelopment in the countryside itself (see Dixon's book on agricultural systems and rural development in this series). Unfortunately successful programmes of this nature either tend to be very expensive or based on socialist co-operative movements, neither of which appeal to poverty-stricken capitalist governments. Many have, therefore, resorted to other less economic responses designed simply to prevent population movement into the already overcrowded cities.

Some of these measures have been variations on the South African pass system, designed to prohibit urban residence to those without official permission. Without draconian police enforcement, such systems have been abject failures, spawning corruption or simply being ignored by people, many of whose informal-sector activities are already illegal anyway.

Slightly more 'successful' have been attempts to deflect or redirect migrants away from large cities to other reception areas. Where newly developed or developable lands exist, as in Indonesia (see case study C) or Malaysia, some success may be achieved, although in small numbers in relation to total migration flows. More effective, at least for a short while, has been the encouragement of potential migrants to move directly overseas to labour-short urban centres abroad. As discussed in chapter 2, this has been a notable feature of certain Mediterranean and former European colonies in the past. It persists today to some extent, although with new destinations and source regions – for example, the huge movement of Mexicans, legally and illegally, into the United States.

Overall, however, government attempts to control and curb rural–urban migration have met with only limited success. Certainly the broadly based rural development schemes needed for effective counter-attractions to the city seem to be beyond the means of most Third World economies. The consequence in so many countries has been to introduce family planning programmes in lieu of, rather than in parallel with, development schemes. This brings the discussion to the question of natural growth.

Natural population growth and the city

In general, cities in the Third World began their recent acceleration of growth under different fertility conditions from those in the west. In contrast to nineteenth-century Europe, death rates had already begun to fall as a result of improved sanitation, medical care and nutrition. Birth rates, in contrast, are subject to a more complex set of social, economic and cultural influences and have remained relatively high, particularly in low-income areas.

The reasons why poor people have large families are quite well known. Children provide security in old age, as well as supplying additional income-earning potential. They do not affect the opportunity costs to women because so many poor women are uneducated and have limited job opportunities. In addition, the extended family system helps share the burden of coping with large numbers of children. Finally, it is claimed that sheer ignorance of the benefits or methods of family planning also contribute to the presence of large families.

All of these arguments in favour of large families relate to individual households. In contrast, those supporting family planning list benefits of a broader societal, economic nature: smaller families lead to more domestic savings and investment, lessen pressure on limited urban resources and improve the human capital resources of the city (small families produce healthier workers). Thus reduced fertility is in the national interest.

Fertility can be influenced by a variety of determinants, but in general these can be grouped into two categories. First are the broad socio-

Transmigration in Indonesia

Between 1961 and 1981 Indonesia's population grew by 60 per cent and most of this increase was in Java which, although it comprises only 7 per cent of the land area, contains 60 per cent of the population of 160 million (figure C.1). Although it is a fertile island, Java cannot sustain annual increases of nearly 2 million people and almost half of its rural population live below the poverty line.

The over-population of Java compared to other islands in the archipelago has long encouraged successive governments to try to alleviate the situation by programmes of planned population shifts. These began in 1905 under the Dutch colonial administration and were continued when Indonesia became independent, but until the 1980s the transmigration schemes had made very little impression on Java's population growth, with the great majority moving to South Sumatra.

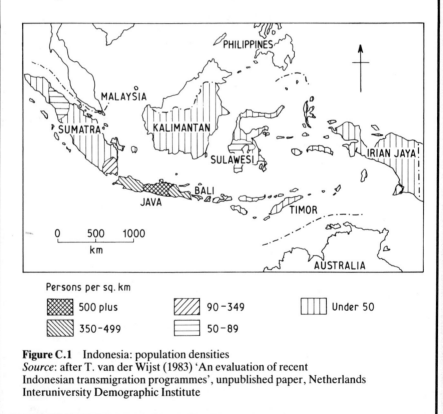

Figure C.1 Indonesia: population densities
Source: after T. van der Wijst (1983) 'An evaluation of recent Indonesian transmigration programmes', unpublished paper, Netherlands Interuniversity Demographic Institute

Within the last two five-year plans, however, there has been a huge acceleration in the transmigration programme (figure C.2). This has followed the Indonesian government's centralization and streamlining of its administration, which has stabilized costs per family, but also owes a great deal to substantial financial support from the World Bank.

Since 1905 approximately 3.5 million people have been moved, almost 70 per cent of those between 1979 and 1984. Over the current five-year plan to 1989 another 4 million are to be encouraged to migrate. Now, however, the target areas have changed and many are being sent to the frontier areas of Kalimantan or Irian Jaya, more for strategic reasons than for development motives.

Despite the recent escalation in numbers, there are continuing problems with the transmigration programme. Many families find that they receive very small plots of land in areas of lower fertility to those they left behind. The hostility of local ethnic and cultural groups, together with poor communications to commercial centres, also makes life difficult for the migrants so that many choose to leave the land and migrate to towns and cities in search of fresh opportunities. Whether intensified national and international investment can prevent this happening must be very doubtful. But Indonesia feels obliged to continue this programme because of the enthusiasm of its major financial supporter, the World Bank, and is fearful that it may lose international credit-worthiness if it does not co-operate.

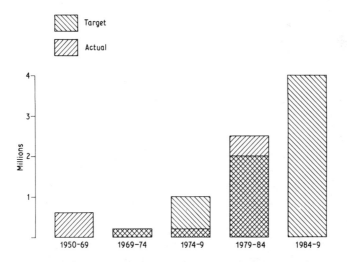

Figure C.2   Indonesia: transmigration targets and achievements

economic changes within society as a whole, and second are the more specific and direct attempts to change fertility at the household level. The former encompass measures which are too extensive and complex to discuss here, such as improved health care, education and employment opportunities (especially for women), all designed to alleviate poverty and redistribute wealth and thus bring about a revaluation of family priorities with regards to children. In short, these measures encourage the sort of change that has already occurred in most developed countries.

Such commitments to basic needs are expensive and long term, so many Third World governments prefer the cheaper, more direct and more immediate measures couched at the household level: for example, raising the minimum legal age for marriage, re-emphasizing breast-feeding of children but, above all, encouraging the adoption of family planning through contraception. In effect, what families in the Third World are being asked to do is to reverse the process that occurred in Europe and North America and voluntarily reduce their family size in order to bring about economic growth. Unfortunately, whilst the poor are expected to make maximum sacrifices in this respect, the economic benefits usually accrue to relatively few who are already wealthy and control the resources which are conserved by population control.

International agencies, perhaps fearful of the political consequences of uncontrolled population growth, have encouraged the adoption of family planning programmes. These are now officially supported by all but the most conservative governments, not only through a series of advisory and incentive schemes but also, in certain countries, by substantial disincentives to large families. In Singapore, for example, families with more than two children receive lower priority in employment, housing and education waiting lists.

Although the main fertility problem still lies in the countryside, it is usually the case that family planning programmes are most effectively deployed in cities. Of course, large numbers of urban poor are characterized by high levels of fertility, for exactly the same reasons as their rural counterparts, but most of the acceptors tend to be middle-income, upwardly mobile families who would be inclined to pursue voluntary curbs to family size in any case. The urban poor, in contrast, are much more likely to 'respond', in terms of fertility, to the more comprehensive, societal changes noted above. But these are unlikely to occur in many countries in the near future.

It is at this point that arguments about urban population growth turn full circle. High rates of growth, whether natural or migrational, are the consequence of development disparities, both social and spatial, not the cause. Yet, over the last decade, overseas aid for general development has fallen, whilst funds specifically tied to the expansion of family planning programmes have increased. As a result the quality of life for many of the urban poor has continued to deteriorate. The next chapter will examine the political response of the poor to their plight.

Key ideas

1 Migrational and natural growth vary in relative importance in different locations but are generally high.
2 Rural–urban migration has changed in character in recent years.
3 Government responses have largely been ineffective in preventing rural–urban migration.
4 High fertility persists in many cities, particularly amongst poor families.

4
Poverty and politics in
Third World cities

Introduction

Previous chapters have painted a vivid picture of the drastic changes that have affected Third World countries in recent years. The move from late colonialism to neo-capitalist exploitation of an increasingly integrated world economy has taken only two or three decades. The focus for much of this change has been the large capital cities. But how have such economic fluctuations been incorporated into urban development and why have the burgeoning masses of urban poor not protested more forcefully against their underprivileged position?

Much of the answer to such questions lies in the form of urban management adopted within the Third World, in which national governments and international agencies (commercial and political) have combined within the guise of the planning process to create a suitable setting for the expansion of global capitalism. An examination of such developments forms the first section of this chapter.

But the reaction of the urban masses to this manipulated urban development has been muted, even when they have been conspicuously neglected. Controversy has raged for many years over the capacity of the urban poor to withstand such exploitation and the second part of this chapter will examine both sides of the argument before looking at some of the ways in which the poor have made their protests against the present system.

The view from the top: urban management of capital cities

Since 1970 the geography of many capital cities in the Third World has been transformed by their national governments in order to facilitate the entry of the multinational corporations and their factories. This has been achieved through three principal means. First, there has been an administrative reorganization to enable national governments to assume the functions of municipal authorities; second, these governments have spent heavily on modernization within the capital cities; and third, the activities of the informal sector have been repressed, particularly where they are in conflict with the modernization process. Although these changes are described below with particular reference to South-east Asia, the trends hold true for many other parts of the Third World.

Administrative reorganization

This has been particularly characteristic of those regions of the Third World where industrialization by western firms has been most rapid. South-east Asia is one such region and within it Singapore has provided a model for successful development that other governments have sought to emulate. Much of Singapore's success was attributed to its being a compact city state organized directly by a national government. Accordingly between 1972 and 1975 four other South-east Asian capital cities, Jakarta, Bangkok, Manila and Kuala Lumpur, were transformed into mini-states on the Singapore model (table 4.1).

All of the new authorities were under the executive control of ministers or governors represented at cabinet level. In each, the outdated master plans were soon replaced by technocratic planning teams using systems analysis, irrespective of the quality of local data. This technocracy, often expatriate in personnel or funding, replaced direct communication with urban populations and was used by ruling cliques to provide pseudo-scientific justification for pre-ordained development objectives. Accountability to urban populations through municipal elections was the exception rather than the rule.

Table 4.1 Capital city–region formation in South-east Asia

	Year	New administrative area	Chief executive
Singapore	1965	—	Prime Minister
Bangkok	1972	Bangkok Metropolitan Area	Governor
Jakarta	1974	Province	Governor
Kuala Lumpur	1974	Federal Territory	Prime Minister
Manila	1975	Metro Manila	Governor

Investment in modernization

One of the development objectives legitimized by the planning technocrats was large-scale investment in the modern corporate sector – visible symbols of progress, such as luxury hotels, conference centres, mass transit systems, all designed to impress foreign investors rather than to raise the living standards of the population as a whole.

Despite this primary objective, there has also been investment in schemes ostensibly aimed at the welfare of the poor, such as low-cost housing projects or minibus services, but the reasons for such action were only thinly linked to welfare considerations. Stronger motivation was either economic, to increase the productivity of the poor by improving their health and getting them to work more quickly; or political, gestures to ease the growing frustrations of the urban poor and forestall insurrection.

Suppressing the informal sector

More indicative of real administrative attitudes towards the urban poor is the attempt of many national governments to suppress or eradicate informal-sector activities. Such activities, whether street trading or constructing squatter housing, have long been anathema to western planners and advisors but attracted increased antagonism because of the competition they posed to expensive modernization schemes. So pedicabs were prohibited in order to encourage people to use the new state-run maxibuses, and hawkers were prosecuted to encourage street-traders to move into the new (licensed) purpose-built markets. The effect of much of this legislation was simply to make the life of the poor that much more difficult and to encourage them to become even more clandestine in their activities.

The urban authorities are aware, however, that the informal sector is of considerable value to the city (this is discussed in more detail in the following chapter). So that although extensive and powerful proscriptive legislation existed on the statute books, this tended to be applied only in periodic bursts. The idea is to control the activities of the informal sector rather than to eliminate it entirely – a move which might well cause violent reaction.

But why have the urban poor not reacted more strongly to the modernization and repression programmes that national governments have implemented in their capital cities? Conflicting opinions exist on this matter and it is worthwhile examining them a little closer.

Case study D

Urban management and political protest in Manila, Philippines

The Philippines were claimed for Spain by Magellan in 1521 and by the 1570s the role of Manila as the primary economic and urban focus of the fragmented country was firmly established. The transfer to the United States in 1899 made little difference to this process so that at present metropolitan Manila contains some six million people and is ten times larger than Davao City, the second ranking urban centre.

Since independence the Philippine government has been in the hands of traditional land-owning families. For the last twenty years the Marcos family were determined to modernize the country and its economy, and regarded the activities of the urban poor as a substantial impediment to progress. Manila, in particular, has been a battleground in this struggle between the state and the poor.

In 1975, following the example of other South-east Asian governments, the capital city-region of Metro Manila was established under the governorship of Imelda Marcos, wife of President Ferdinand Marcos, and also Minister for Human Settlements. Immediately a major World Bank planning analysis was undertaken and a series of major investments in urban development were instigated. These clearly illustrated the westernization favoured by the Marcos regime. The first comprised an International Convention Centre built at a cost of US$150 million to house a World Bank conference. Another US$360 million was loaned by government agencies for the construction of fourteen new hotels to accommodate the delegates at the conference. To put this in perspective, in the same year, 1976, only US$13 million was allocated for government housing construction.

The poor did receive direct attention in the context of these investments but only in the sense that squatter settlements in the vicinity of the centre, the hotels or the road from the airport, were demolished in a well-publicized 'beautification' programme. It is estimated that some 60,000 squatters lost their homes before the World Bank conference and a further 100,000 prior to the Miss World pageant the following year.

Even ostensible measures to assist the poor were affected by the élitist control of urban planning and the desire for it to achieve national objectives. In 1976 an international competition was held to design an innovative plan for rehousing some 3500 squatters from the large Tondo squatter area (figure D.1) at nearby Dagat Dagatan.

Imelda Marcos claimed that this would be a prototype for rehousing squatters throughout the world, publicizing it widely at the United Nations

Case study D (*continued*)

Habitat meeting held in the same year. The real goal, however, was to get rid of the squatters in order to extend the city's port area. But the main criticism was of the scheme itself which was totally élitist in concept and organization. Competing firms were provided with information in the form of booklets, maps and data but no direct consultation with the squatters themselves was suggested, planned or expected.

In competing for the generous prize money of US$100,000 and the construction contract, many firms produced worthy plans which concentrated on housing and environmental improvements, with abundant innovative energy-saving technology. Far less attention was paid to the provision of

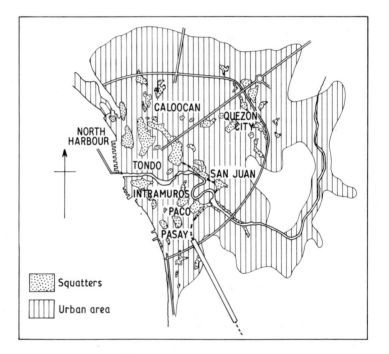

Figure D.1   Manila: main squatter districts
Source: updated to *c*. 1980 from M. Juppenlatz (1970) *Cities in Transformation*, St Lucia, University of Queensland Press.

Case study D (*continued*)

jobs, land rights, education and health care on which the squatters themselves placed much higher priority. Needless to say, progress on the resettlement scheme has been expensive, limited and unpopular.

During this particular episode the squatters themselves made some effective public protests against the high-handed action of the Marcos government. Much of this effectiveness was due to their being organized into a city-wide organization, the Ugnayan, which is relatively rare amongst low-income urban communities, given their fragmented nature and interests. Once the national government took over the management of the city, this effectiveness was challenged by direct replacement of *barrios* leaders by government appointees whose loyalties were upwards to their employers rather than downwards to their *barangay* communities. Major Ugnayan leaders were arrested and prevented from attending the Habitat conference at which Imelda Marcos outlined her resettlement plans.

It was the continuation of such high-handed urban management that contributed substantially to the downfall of the Marcos regime, alienating not only the poor but also the middle class, and eventually exhausting the patience of overseas supporters too.

Political protest and the poor

The revolutionary poor

The underprivileged condition of so many urban dwellers in the Third World has long encouraged observers to assume the existence of a great suppressed potential for revolutionary change. For example, in the mid 1960s Barbara Ward, Professor of International Economics at Columbia University wrote of

the unskilled poor streaming away from subsistence agriculture to exchange the squalor of rural poverty for the even deeper miseries of the shantytown . . . everywhere undermining the all to frail structure of public order and thus retarding the economic development that can alone help their plight . . . there is enough explosive material to produce in the world at large the pattern of a bitter class conflict . . . threatening, ultimately, the security of the comfortable west.

Such comments were not untypical at the time, arising from the concern of modernization strategists that western-style development had failed to bring the predicted widespread benefits. And yet in the twenty years since Barbara Ward made her statement, only rarely have urban masses participated in a revolutionary change of government, for example in Iran, Nicaragua and the Philippines.

Most of the anti-colonial independence struggles were rural-based precisely because colonial strength rested in the large towns and, whilst it is true that there have been many urban-based changes of government in independent Third World states, most of these have been 'palace' coups of which the masses were seldom even spectators.

Given this lack of involvement of the urban poor, some observers sought to explain the situation by suggesting that two distinct groups existed. The first comprised the 'rising poor', those in regular employment who have much to lose and nothing to gain from violent upheaval. Such people tend to be apolitical or given to compromise. The second group are the lumpen proletariat – the recent migrants, living in the shanty towns, who have no regular income and whose traditional culture ties and stability have been broken. To many, including the revolutionary writer Franz Fanon, such men comprised 'one of the most spontaneous and radical revolutionary forces'.

However, this was not borne out by reality and, was very much the consequence of the limited understanding of the period. What was not appreciated until the 1970s was the important role of the informal sector in enabling the urban poor to 'get by' and hope for improvements in the future. Indeed, as research and knowledge of this area of activities increased, so a strong body of opinion grew that the urban poor were quite conservative.

The conservative poor

Many of the early investigations of the urban poor in the late 1960s and early 1970s analysed their voting patterns and concluded that they voted more conservatively than the middle classes. Although it must be cautioned that in many cities relatively few of the poor are enfranchised and those who might be more radical by inclination would tend not to cast a vote. Despite such caveats, however, there was general agreement with John Turner who described squatter areas as potential 'urban safety belts'.

Such conservatism is not an innate quality of the poor, although many do have aspirations for themselves and their children and prefer not to jeopardize their future. However, most poor communities are strongly influenced by conservative leaders. Many of these are religious leaders, although, as the boxed case study of Manila indicates, some religious leaders can be quite militant. More consistently conservative in this respect are the small businessmen to whom most poor households are frequently in debt and for whom they will vote or behave as directed.

The realist position

It is clear, therefore, that it is inappropriate to label the urban poor *en masse* as conservative or revolutionary. They are drawn into the urban political system in a variety of ways and are subject to many different influencing forces. Within this complex network, they enter into what political activity they feel to be appropriate.

It might be useful at this point to clarify what 'political movement' means in the context of the Third World. For most of the urban poor it would not relate only to formal political participation, in elections, for example, but would also encompass any activity designed to influence the redistribution of scarce resources, much of which could be quite informal. A further useful distinction is that between public and private political action, whether an open confrontation with the authorities takes place or not. Many revolutionary movements require a much higher profile than most of the poor are prepared to take, preferring to challenge the authorities at a low-key level. If these two distinguishing features are combined (figure 4.1), the range of possible political actions by the urban poor becomes clearly evident. The more institutionalized options are often the least effective form of action. As we have noted, voting tends to be confined to an enfranchised few who often cast their votes as recommended by their community leader. Trade

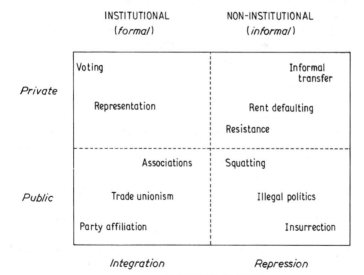

Figure 4.1   Types of political action by the urban poor

unions too can be very ineffective vehicles for political protest by the poor, few of whom have the sort of employment which leads to union membership. Indeed, in many cities waged, unionized employees form a labour élite whose organizations act more in the protective capacity of medieval guilds than as modern trade unions.

As a result of this ineffectiveness, many of the urban poor have recourse to less 'acceptable' methods of involvement. As we have seen, only occasionally would this encompass open insurrection but many are prepared to take public action on a more personal level to gain access to essential resources they would otherwise be denied. The most visible type of action in this context is perhaps the seizure of land by squatters. Although many urban authorities claim that such action is encouraged by radical political parties, there is much evidence to show that initial moves are the result of personal motivation and that only when threatened with subsequent eviction does more overt political organization occur.

But the most common form of political action by the poor is simply to use whatever means they can to cope with an unequal system. In this sense the entire informal sector with its illegal and semi-legal living and working environment constitutes a form of political protest (see following chapter).

One inescapable fact about the urban poor in the Third World is that their numbers are continuing to grow rapidly. The question raised by this is to what extent the various coping mechanisms of the informal sector will continue to circumvent more extreme reaction to worsening deprivation. In some Third World countries, such as India, Turkey or Colombia, violence is becoming increasingly frequent as those born into urban poverty become less tolerant of continued exploitation. Will they light the blue touch paper to the urban explosion that those such as Barbara Ward have feared for so long?

Key ideas

1 In many capital cities urban management has been taken over by national governments.
2 Urban planning is structured to meet goals of modernization.
3 Political control of the urban masses is maintained by limited investment in basic needs to ease frustrations.
4 The urban poor cannot be uniformly classified as revolutionary or conservative.
5 Political protest takes various forms, the most common of which is simply coping with inequality through the informal sector.

5
Employment in the city

Introduction

As noted in chapter 1 there is a clear relationship between economic growth and urbanization, although the nature of that relationship is the subject of intense debate. Nevertheless, almost all development strategists, whether Marxist or capitalist, identify industrialization as the key to economic growth, and this focuses investment on the city rather than the countryside. The disagreement arises over the type of industrialization to be promoted. Some argue for heavy industry, others for light manufacturing; some support import-substitution, others export-orientation; some favour capital-intensive investment, others labour-intensive.

Whatever the type of industrial programme followed or the national income derived from this, it is uncommon to find the majority of urban residents incorporated into this type of employment. Indeed, for much of the urban labour force the prospect of regular waged employment is small and they must obtain what income they can within what has become popularly known as the informal sector.

This chapter will examine both of these important urban economic sectors, beginning with industrialization, and accompany each with a case study to illustrate their relative importance in real world situations. A broader examination of the role of industrialization in the Third World can be found in Chandra's book in this series.

Industrialization and urban employment

The background to growth

We have already noted in earlier chapters that development in the Third World is unlikely to follow a similar path to that of the west and yet for many years this is what development strategists suggested should be the case. Hence the interest in industrial investment. In the colonial past, of course, there had been little interest in the promotion of industry in the colonies. In fact, in countries such as India, local competition to European manufacturing was closed down. But in the years immediately following independence there was very little money available for investment in Third World industry. Indeed, as we have seen in chapter 3, labour began to migrate to established areas of production in Europe.

Nevertheless many countries attempted to begin import-substitution programmes, raising high protective tariffs to produce consumer goods hitherto imported in order to save valuable foreign exchange. Unfortunately in many countries the domestic markets were not large enough to sustain this production, which itself needed expensive imported capital equipment, fuel and even materials in order to commence production. The cost of the finished goods was usually higher than that of those originally imported.

However, temporary problems of this nature were accepted as part of the early price of establishing independent industrial production and in the 1960s the industrial output of the Third World rose by an average of 7 per cent per annum. This was very favourable compared to many developed countries. Much of this early growth was, perhaps surprisingly, in heavy industry rather than in the textiles often associated with the Third World.

Once again, however, disaggregation of the data reveals considerable variation in the pattern of growth. First, it varied through time, with many countries experiencing an early spurt followed by stagnation and recession. Second, it varied across geographical space, with some countries experiencing more rapid and sustained growth than others. Such trends have become even more marked in the period since the 1970s which, as noted in chapter 2, has been marked by considerable investment by multinational corporations into selected cities in the Third World.

Although cheap labour has been an important factor in this investment shift, it is not the countries of cheapest labour that have benefited. After all, most products must compete on a world market and so the production process itself needs to be fairly sophisticated. Experienced labour is preferred, as are countries with useful local resources and good export facilities. In addition, those locations that are strategically important to the west have been able to attract large investments from individual western countries and from the multilateral agencies such as the World Bank. Mexico, Brazil, Taiwan and, until recently, Iran are all countries that have benefited in this way. Over the years, however, interstate aid has been supplemented and supplanted by multinational corporation investment and, most recently, by finance capital (from banks, insurance companies and the like).

Newly industrializing countries

Large-scale industrialization has, therefore, occurred only in about ten countries (table 5.1) and several of these are European. There are surprisingly few common denominators to account for economic growth in these Newly Industrializing Countries (NICS), as they are known, apart from their political value to the west and their strong and obtrusive state governments which have encouraged the inflow, and affected the internal allocation, of investment funds. To consider NICS such as Hong Kong and Singapore as bastions of free-wheeling *laissez-faire* capitalism is very naïve.

In other ways the NICS vary enormously – in population size (and therefore labour force and domestic market); in primary source of investment funds (in Taiwan, South Korea and Hong Kong this has often been domestic, elsewhere it is largely foreign); and in their entrepreneurial tradition. The one important feature which draws all these economies together is their commitment to large-scale, export-based industrialization strategies as a means to economic growth. Such strategies aim to overcome import costs and foreign exchange by massive exports of commodities that can be produced cheaply through the use of abundant local resources – all too often this means human resources.

Table 5.1 New industrializing countries 1984

	Population (m)	Population growth rate (% p.a.) 1974–84	GNP p.c. (US$)	GNP p.c. growth rate (% p.a.) 1965–84	Manufacturing as % GDP	Exports as % GDP
Brazil	130.0	2.3	1,880	5.0	27	8
Mexico	75.0	2.9	2,240	3.2	22	20
Hong Kong	5.5	2.5	6,000	6.2	22	96
Singapore	2.5	1.3	6,620	7.8	24	176
South Korea	40.0	1.6	2,010	6.7	27	37
Taiwan*	18.0	1.9	1,600	8.5	35	52
Greece	9.8	1.1	3,920	4.0	18	19
Portugal	10.1	1.1	2,230	3.7	37	32
Yugoslavia	22.8	0.8	2,570	4.7	31	30
Spain	38.2	1.0	4,780	3.0	25	18

Note: * data up to 1980 only.
Source: World Bank (1986) *World Development Report.*

As noted earlier, these export products must compete in world markets and be of high quality. Factories and production processes are thus fairly sophisticated and need high capital investment and advanced production technologies. Almost all of these are imported through the medium of the multinational corporation, although once a substantial body of local plant, expertise, capital and skill is built up, it is possible for domestic generation of continued development, as has occurred in Hong Kong for example, which now has its own multinational firms and investment-financial corporations.

Table 5.2   The impact of industrialization in developed and developing countries

	Value added (%)		Labour force (%)	
	Developed countries 1880	Developing countries 1960	Developed countries 1880	Developing countries 1960
Agriculture	33.0	38.4	56.2 (0.4)	70.7 (1.1)
Industry	24.2	22.8	24.1 (2.1)	11.5 (3.8)
Mining/quarrying			1.7	0.6
Manufacturing			18.8	8.9
Construction			5.0	2.0
Services	42.7	38.8	19.5 (2.1)	17.8 (3.9)

Note: Figures in brackets refer to rates of growth 1880–1900, 1960–70.
Source: L. Squires (1981) *Employment Policy in Developing Countries*, Washington DC, World Bank.

Whichever industrialization strategy, or mix of strategies, is chosen one important factor must be appreciated, i.e. that, although the manufacturing impact on Gross Domestic Product (GDP) may be substantial, its impact on employment is often much more limited, certainly more limited than in developed countries during the early stages of their industrialization process (table 5.2). This confirms the fact that in many Third World countries the manufacturing sector is relatively highly capitalized, as is productivity per worker. This has given rise to what some observers have called a 'labour aristocracy' of relatively well-paid, privileged workers. Despite the reputation that multinational factories have for employing cheap labour, wages are often higher than for many other sectors of the urban workforce and certainly far higher than the incomes received in the informal sector (table 5.3), although this will vary according to the male:female ratio in the labour force.

Table 5.3 Java: wage levels and working conditions in foreign and domestic firms

	Weaving					Kretek cigarettes			
	Foreign	Domestic							
		Mechanized			Non-mechanized				
		Large	Med.	Small		V. large	Large	Med.	Small
Number of firms	6	8	15	10	11	2	7	6	4
Average number of workers	1,022	1,068	276	62	11	19,692	2,126	299	57
Average monthly wage (Rp)*	17,000	10,000	5,300	5,300	3,700	10,000	5,100	3,800	2,100
Fringe benefits	good		poor		none	moderate			none
Conditions of work	good		poor	very poor	poor			very poor	
Reliability of work	regular		moderate		erratic	moderate		erratic	
Labour turnover	low		low		high	low		high	
Absenteeism	low		moderate		high	moderate		high	

Note: * Rp 900 = £1.
Source: C. Manning (1977) *The Life of the Poor in Indonesian Cities*, Clayton, Monash University Press.

Singapore

Singapore is a very young country, achieving republic status only in 1965. Since then its economy has grown very rapidly and in Asia ranks second only to Japan in terms of prosperity (table E.1). However, in 1965 prospects seemed bleak as the withdrawal of the British undermined the stability of regional trade and removed the major contribution that defence made to the economy. In addition, there was massive in-migration of Chinese from neighbouring countries and a high birth rate.

The Peoples Action Party, headed by Lee Kuan Yew who is still Prime Minister, decided on an aggressive export-based industrial growth financed by foreign investment, rightly believing that this would lead to some international protection for the small, new and politically vulnerable nation. It was also felt that overseas companies would bring technical expertise, create many jobs and provide direct access to overseas markets. In its turn the Singapore government was prepared to offer financial incentives and to guarantee a cheap and controlled labour force.

Social programmes were therefore used to create political stability amongst a very mixed ethnic population (77 per cent of the present 2.5 million are Chinese, 15 per cent are Malays, Indians form 6 per cent and others 2 per cent). A massive low-cost housing programme was started which subsequently led to the creation of extensive 'new towns' and now accommodates 70 per cent of the population, many of whom own their own homes and thus have a vested interest in being responsible citizens. Other stabilizing measures included the state control of trade unions, the introduction of birth and immigration control programmes and the demolition of the slum districts that once housed the radical Chinese opposition parties (plate E.1).

As in most Third World countries, foreign companies were offered a range of fiscal incentives to invest in Singapore, many of which were focused on the export-processing zone in the new town of Jurong (figure E.1). Over 60 per cent of all manufacturing jobs are now located here, its importance being enhanced by the creation of massive container docks nearby. Much of the industrial growth was financed by United States and Japanese capital and was particularly vigorous in oil-refining, ship-building and repairing, and the manufacture of textiles, plastics and electrical products.

The world recession and the rising costs of its own labour, compared with other South-east Asian countries, began to curtail growth in all of these manufacturing sectors by the early 1980s; tourism too was affected by a downturn in arrivals. But, before these changes occurred, Singapore had already begun to reshape its economy by a shift into what the government

Case study E (*continued*)

Table E.1 Singapore: selected indicators of development, 1983

	Singapore	Malaysia	Thailand	Philippines	Indonesia	Hong Kong	Taiwan*	South Korea	Japan
Population (m)	2.5	14.9	49.2	52.1	156.7	5.3	18.2	40.0	119.4
Pop. growth rate p.a. (1973–83)	1.3	2.4	2.3	2.7	2.3	2.5	1.9	1.6	0.9
GNP p.c. (US$)	6,620	1,860	820	760	560	6,000	2,720	2,010	10,120
GNP p.c. Growth rate p.a. (1965–83)	7.8	4.3	4.3	2.8	5.0	6.2	8.5	6.6	4.8
Manufacturing % of GDP	24	19	19	25	13	22	35	27	30
Services % of GDP	62	44	50	42	35	69	NA	47	95
Growth in manufacturing (1965–73)	19.5	NA	11.4	8.5	9.0	NA	22.1	21.1	13.6
Growth in manufacturing (1973–83)	7.9	10.6	8.9	5.0	12.6	NA	12.8	11.8	6.6
Inflation rate p.a. (1973–83)	4.5	6.5	8.7	11.7	18.0	9.9	NA	19.3	4.7

Note: *data to 1980 only.
NA = not available.

Key Sources: World Bank (1985) *World Development Report*; G. Jones (1983) 'Economic growth and changing female employment structure in the cities of Southeast and East Asia', unpublished paper, Department of Demography, Australian National University; *Far Eastern Economic Review* (1983–5); Department of Statistics, Singapore (1982) *Economic and Social Indicators*, Singapore Government Press.

called a 'second industrial revolution'. This is based on high-skill, high-technology industries, once again firmly focused in terms of urban location into a science park adjoining the new National University.

Accompanying this technological change has been a determined attempt to make Singapore into a major financial centre for investment in South and East Asia. Given its reputation for political stability and sound fiscal policies, Singapore has proved a relatively popular location for the new *compradores* of capital, the international banks, insurance and other finance

Plate E.1 Singapore: demolition of old slum tenements to make way for the expansion of the new central business district

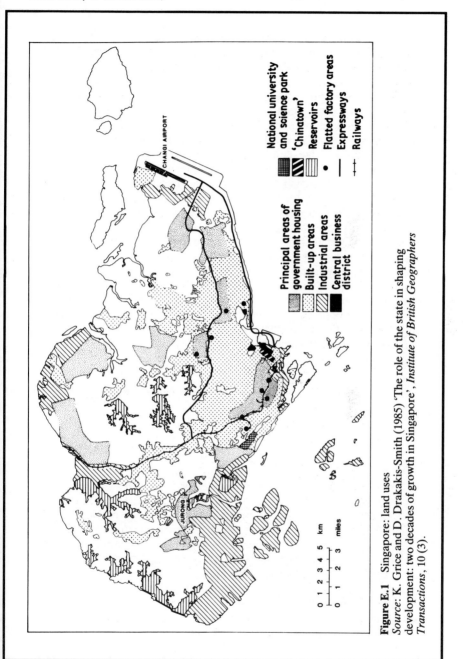

Figure E.1 Singapore: land uses
Source: K. Grice and D. Drakakis-Smith (1985) 'The role of the state in shaping
development: two decades of growth in Singapore', *Institute of British Geographers
Transactions*, 10 (3).

houses, which have quickly taken up the space provided by the demolition of the inner-city 'chinatown' slums to produce a new business district skyline akin to that of New York or Los Angeles.

Until the benefits of these changes take full effect, the recession has been countermanded in the short term by bringing forward a massive programme of government construction – not only in public housing but also in airport redevelopment and an extensive mass-transit system. Typically, however, the government has also sought to increase social control over its citizens in order to create the high-standard labour-force needed to sustain the second industrial revolution. Singapore's people are now virtually instructed on how many children they may have, what language they must speak, which schools they may go to, and where they can live and work. In these circumstances there is obviously a social price to pay for economic success. The extensive degree of control that the Singapore government exerts over economic and social change in the republic clearly indicates that so-called *laissez-faire*, free-market economies are nothing of the sort.

Despite these draconian efforts 1985 saw the growth rate of the Singapore economy slump to near zero for the first time ever. In the most recent election growing disillusion with the authoritarian government was reflected in the fact that opposition candidates, although capturing only 2 of 79 seats, polled one-third of the popular vote. Whether such changes are the herald of a longer downturn in the fortunes of the city-state, or even of other NICs, remains to be seen.

Impact on the city

In terms of location the manufacturing sector tends to be concentrated into the larger cities, particularly the capital. For example, Taipei has one-third of Taiwan's industrial establishments of more than 500 employees, whilst Manila contains 79 per cent of the Philippines manufacturing employment. However, although smaller cities are less important in absolute terms, they still contain a consistently high proportion of manufacturing jobs (table 5.4), although smaller firms are likely to be more predominant within this pattern. For example, one study in Davao City, the second largest city in the Philippines, found that no less than 759 of the 807 industrial firms employed less than 10 people, 36 employed between 10 and 100, whilst the remaining 12 had more than 100 workers each and between them employed some 40 per cent of the industrial labour force.

Table 5.4   South Korea: manufacturing employment and city size

Size category	No. of cities	Average population (m)	Manufacturing employment (%) City workforce	National workforce
Capital	1	6.9	34.5	35.1
500,000 and over	5	1.1	30.3	28.0
250,000–499,999	4	0.3	27.8	5.3
100,000–249,999	18	0.2	22.9	8.5
60,000–99,999	9	0.08	18.9	1.5
Smaller centres and rural areas				21.6

Source: D. Rondinelli (1982) 'Intermediate cities in developing countries', *Third World Planning Review* 4(4).

Figures such as these indicate the importance of the smaller, often entirely indigenous firms in urban employment, if not in terms of output. The United Nations (UNIDO) has calculated that small-scale 'modern' plants contribute about one-quarter of manufacturing value added but more than half of the industrial employment. This, of course, would only encompass small firms in the modern sector of the economy for which data is available; many more people are employed in the unrecorded activities of the informal sector, the products of which circulate throughout urban markets as a whole. In India, for example, it is reported that 78 per cent of the industrial labour force was engaged in the 'non-modern' sector (see Chandra in this series).

Within the city, the distribution of industry is often closely related to size of plant. Smaller factories may be scattered throughout the urban area but tend to be clustered around the central business district where they often blend indistinguishably into more informal and illegal enterprises. In cities where space is at a premium, such as Hong Kong or Singapore, flatted factories have been constructed, giving multiple levels subdivided into different units occupying whole or part floors. However, in most of the rapidly industrializing cities of the Third World, the larger multinational factories tend to be concentrated in major estates, usually adjacent to port areas, in which special financial incentives are available to encourage foreign investment. Such estates, known as free-trade zones, export-processing zones or special-processing zones, have proliferated over the last two decades, even in such non-capitalist countries as China (figure 5.1). In morphological terms such zones are the fulcrum of capitalist exploitation of the Third World, containing as they do predominantly female labour (see also chapter 6).

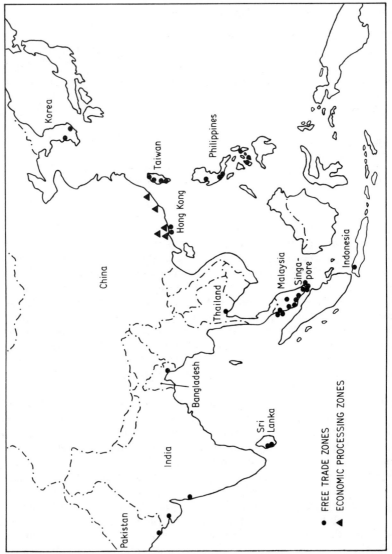

Figure 5.1 Asia: the distribution of export processing zones

The informal or petty-commodity sector
The growth of a concept

Despite the very wide use of the term 'informal sector', the concept is relatively recent and has been widely accepted only since the mid 1970s. Its origins lay in the 1930s when, even then, some investigators were claiming that western development was not absorbing the traditional economy but was simply existing side-by-side in a dual system. This idea of dualism was taken up again in the late 1960s by researchers who could see that the modernization or 'similar path' development strategies were not benefiting large numbers of the urban poor. Once it was realized that many people lived in permanent poverty and yet remained politically docile, several people began to investigate more closely their lifestyle to see how they survived in the city.

What followed was a series of investigations which began to build up the character of this lifestyle, primarily within the field of economic activities. Table 5.5 summarizes these characteristics and contrasts them with those of the formal sector – by the mid 1970s the term informal/formal sector coined by Hart had superseded earlier alternative terminology such as bazaar/firm sector, lower/upper circuits or traditional/modern activities.

Most writers emphasized the self-contained nature of the informal sector, the way in which it used small-scale, even recycled, materials to produce, often illegally, small items that sold cheaply to the urban poor themselves. Not only did the informal sector encompass manufacturing but also all other aspects of life for the poor, including services such as preparing and selling

Table 5.5   Formal and informal sector characteristics

Informal sector	Formal sector
Ease of entry	Difficult entry
Indigenous inputs predominate	Overseas inputs
Family property predominates	Corporate property
Small scale of activity	Large scale of activity
Labour-intensive	Capital-intensive
Adapted technology	Imported technology
Skills from outside school system	Formally acquired (often expatriate) skills
Unregulated/competitive market	Protected markets (e.g. tariffs, quotas, licensing arrangements)

Source: C. Rogerson (1985) *The First Decade of Informal Sector Studies*, Environmental Studies Occasional Paper 25.

Plate 5.1   Bangkok: a hawker selling cooled pieces of fruit

cooked foods (plate 5.1), education, traditional health-care and, perhaps most obvious, the construction of squatter housing, all apparently meeting the needs of the low-income groups and operating outside the control of the authorities.

In the late 1970s it became almost fashionable to investigate informal sector activities, with many studies directing their attention towards squatters and their settlements. Given its extent and internal variation, however, it is very difficult to build up a generalized picture of the informal sector, and even less possible or practical to produce statistical summaries of its extent or importance. In some of the capital cities of the poorer Third World countries almost 90 per cent of the working population may be linked to the informal sector, but even in relatively wealthy ones there is often still a high degree of involvement. The streets of Hong Kong, for example, are full of small-scale artisans, traders and retailers, despite its reputation for sophisticated industrial exports (plate 5.2).

What impressd these observers was the apparent self-contained nature of the informal sector. Instead of the urban poor being a hindrance to urban economic expansion, it was seen to be very productive with the urban poor using their considerable energies to meet their own needs, and even some of those of the non-poor, at little cost to the urban authorities. In short, the poor housed, fed and clothed themselves with little government help and yet provided a ready, on-the-spot labour supply for expanding formal sector activities.

Evaluating the informal sector

Despite their vitality, the urban poor were still poor, many even destitute, and, in the eyes of many capitalists, still posed a potential threat to the stability of continued growth and prosperity. Some observers viewed the informal sector as a valuable way of easing the immediate frustrations of the poor by using their energies, together with small-scale assistance or training, to try to help them improve their circumstances in some way. It is this approach which has spawned the so-called basic needs strategy to development, viz. aided self-help programmes which have spread enormously in the 1980s due to the willingness of the United Nations and World Bank to link financial assistance to such schemes. In essence, however, the long-

Plate 5.2   Hong Kong: alley-way artisans in a crowded tenement district

term goal of economic prosperity through western-style modernization was unchanged, and such improvements in basic needs have been criticized for simply easing short-term problems but leaving most of the poor with little more than they had before – merely the acceptable face of capitalism in the Third World.

Indeed, in the late 1970s and the 1980s many of the studies of the informal sector concentrated on revealing its utility not only to the poor, which was already well known, but also to individuals and enterprises in the formal sector. In short, researchers began to realize that the informal sector was not self-contained at all but was linked to the rest of the urban economy in a highly exploitative way. As Rod Burgess has remarked, those in the informal sector 'have not escaped capitalism, they are merely in another part of it'.

Much of the more recent research, therefore, revealed just how difficult it is to actually identify what and who constitute the informal sector as such. A large range of jobs, from busking, to selling, to servicing, are found both in the formal and informal sectors, and it is often the lack of an official licence that classifies the activity, not its organization or function. This means that household income can, and usually does, come from varied sources if its members work in different sectors, making comparative estimates of the income generated by the two sectors quite difficult.

This criticism can also extend to individuals who may change their residential and work patterns many times during their lifetime, or even on an annual, monthly or daily basis. It is especially true of women who drift between domestic, informal and formal activities more fluidly and frequently than men. Indeed, many women who have part-time factory work, cook food for other family members to sell on the streets and undertake normal domestic work, spend each day in three sectors.

These critical studies also pointed out that the informal sector could not be exclusively associated with poverty since many occupations provided incomes higher than those received in the lower-paid formal sector jobs, such as cleaners, night-watchmen and the like. The highest incomes were, however, more likely to be due to lengthy hours of work and accumulated experience rather than to education or status. These jobs, such as pedicab driving, were highly valued and protected through occupational associations that closely controlled entry and numbers (in contrast to the early assumption contained in table 5.5).

As a result of these criticisms, it was recognized that the formal and informal sectors were rather crude conceptual buckets which had drawn valuable attention to the positive values and contribution of the urban poor but which had failed to place them within the perspective of exploitation by groups in the rest of the urban economy. But exactly how does this exploitation occur?

Pondoks and pedlars in Jakarta*

Petty trading, or informal-sector activities, in Jakarta is centred around *pondoks*. These are dwellings where the traders live and obtain their equipment and materials. However, they are not employees but self-employed residents of a sort of lodging house specifically for migrant traders in certain occupations who periodically return to their villages in rural Java. The pondok is run by a *tauke* who is a cross between a landlady and an entrepreneur.

The pondok in this case study is run by a lady called Ibu Mus and its residents/workers all come from the same village and specialize in ice-cream making. The building is made of bamboo and various scavenged materials, and measures only 24 m² but is home for some fifteen people. Lea Jellinek who lived nearby and studied this pondok takes up the story:

> Life in the Mus household began at 4 a.m. when Ibu Mus and her husband Pok Manto received the day's delivery of ice . . . . After the ice had been loaded into the cold storage they divided up the ice-cream ingredients which Ibu Mus had bought at the market the previous day. . . . Whilst Mus and Manto sat on the ground floor weighing out the ingredients (for each trader), the rest of the *pondok* awoke and began to descend the rickety ladder down to the ground. . . . It was about 7 a.m. when they started rotating their buckets of ice-cream and they would sit there twisting and turning for the next three hours or so.
>
> Ibu Mus turned to her own work after she had finished weighing out the ice-cream ingredients. She carefully poured a variety of herbal medicines that she had prepared the previous evening into thirteen well-washed Johnnie Walker bottles . . . and by 6.30 a.m. set out to sell them. Ibu Sajum, Manto's sister-in-law, usually returned from market at the time Ibu Mus was setting out on her rounds and began to dice and cook the vast quantity of food she had brought back from market.
>
> It was still only 7 a.m. The ten ice-cream traders sat in a row mixing their ice-cream. Sajum was busy cooking. Manto occupied himself with all sorts of chores. Often Manto went to market and returned with an assortment of fresh fruit which he chopped into attractive little pieces and placed some ice fragments on top of them. When they were cold he would take them out on the streets to sell. But . . . on most days he devoted his talents to maintaining the ice-cream carts or carrying out alterations or repairs on the house.
>
> At about 10 a.m. the ice-cream was ready. Each trader tasted his product and made any final adjustments that he felt were necessary.

Sometimes he asked his colleagues for their opinions and at other times he offered a sample to the group of children from the neighbourhood who invariably congregated when the ice-cream was nearing completion in the hope that their judgement would be called upon. When the product had been approved, the ice-cream bucket was carefully lifted into a push cart and surrounded by a fresh combination of salt and ice. Then, one by one, the traders strode into the kitchen, stripped and washed themselves (then) changed into clean singlets and shorts and sat down to the breakfast that Sajum had prepared.

But the breakfast had only been a small part of Sajum's cooking. She had produced a vast mound of fried savouries and titbits which she now neatly arranged on trays. Then she too changed into a traditional village sarong and kebaja and set off to sell her savouries. Soon everyone else followed suit. One by one the ice-cream traders manoeuvered their carts out of the narrow door of the *pondok*.

Ibu Sajum had a regular clientele. Most of her customers worked in a big government office in Jakarta. They were the sweepers, messenger boys, guards and tea-makers. The office Sajum visited had its own staff cafeteria and traders were not welcome because they deprived the cafeteria of business. But Sajum sold cheaper food cooked in a traditional style and it was much in demand.

The ice-cream traders too had a regular route. The traders from Mus's *pondok* respected one another's territory and did not steal customers from each other. But, of course, they had to compete with the ice-cream sellers from other *pondoks*. Sajum's customers were buying their regular meal but the demand for ice-cream was rather more capricious and varied with the weather and the taste of the traders' ice-cream.

The traders had invested a lot of money and labour into their ice-cream. As it was perishable and could not be refrozen, they could not afford to return to the *pondok* until their stocks had been completely sold. They usually kept to the narrow back streets of the kampung, although the temptation of the major roads was always there. There were throngs of people out on the roads and many of them had rather more to spend than the people who crowded the back streets of the kampung. But there was a campaign against mobile traders and those who succumbed to the lure of the major roads risked losing not just their stalls, but even worse, their carts and all their equipment.

As Sajum and the ice-cream traders were beginning their rounds Ibu Mus's was drawing to an end. She too followed a constant route and in most places found regular customers for her herbal medicines which

Case study F (*continued*)

promised to combat a variety of ills ranging from infertility to unfaithfulness. . . . If any of Mus's wealthier customers mentioned that they had some unwanted old clothing, Mus offered to relieve them of it and if by chance others wanted to borrow money or buy some batik [cloth], Mus offered to help them with those needs as well.

By noon Ibu Mus returned home. She emptied out and thoroughly washed her thirteen Johnnie Walker bottles and stood them upside down to dry. Then she sat down to a meal which Sajum had left for her. When she had finished eating Mus set off for market. She returned with food for the evening meal which she prepared and cooked so that a meal would be ready whenever the ice-cream traders returned. When that was done she set off for the market again, this time to buy all the ingredients for the next day's ice-cream trade that she had been unable to carry on her earlier trip to the market. Mus found much to do about the house after the shopping was over. She carefully folded and stored away the old clothes she had collected. Later she would sell them in her village where they would fetch a fair price at festive times when the villagers felt they had to appear in a new, or at least different, set of clothing. Mus also collected any left over bread from the ice-cream traders who offered it to their customers as an alternative to ice-cream cones. Mus dried the bread in the sun and stored it away in glass jars. This too would fetch a reasonable price in the village when food was in short supply. By four in the afternoon Sajum returned from her food-selling and the two women set off together to collect instalments on the batik Mus had sold on credit as well as the money she loaned at an interest rate of 30 per cent per month!

From 6 p.m. onwards the ice-cream traders began to return. They looked exhausted as they pushed their way through the door of the *pondok* and parked their empty carts inside. They had started work at seven that morning and, if business was slow, it might be 9 p.m. or later before they began to make their way back home. Each trader unloaded and cleaned his cart and then silently consumed the meal Ibu Mus had prepared before climbing up into the attic and going off to sleep. They had neither the time nor the energy for socialising. The next day's ice would be delivered in a few hours and their work would begin all over again.

* This case study is extracted from chapter 6 of *Food, Shelter and Transport in Southeast Asia and the Pacific* (1978), edited by P.J. Rimmer, D. Drakakis-Smith and T.G. McGee, Canberra, Australian National University.

Exploitation of petty-commodity production

The term 'informal sector' has become less popular in recent years because it implies a self-containedness that does not really exist. Most researchers now refer to petty-commodity or petty-capitalist production which more accurately reflects the subordinate or controlled nature of the activities. Nevertheless, the old terminology is still widely used because of familiarity or convenience.

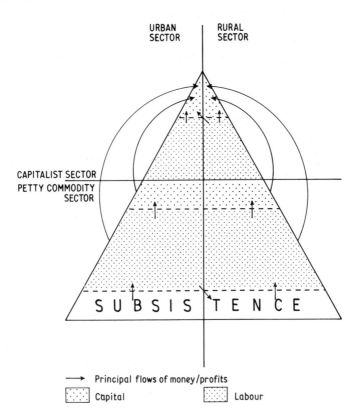

Figure 5.2   Urban petty economy sector links

Figure 5.2 indicates the links between petty-commodity production and the rest of the urban economy, and also to the rural economy. The principal characteristics of each are listed briefly below.

1   Rural subsistence supplies some of the raw materials and much of the food consumed by those in petty-commodity activities. In return a large proportion of accumulated savings is remitted to the rural areas where it is vital for preserving landholdings.

2   Urban subsistence activity also supplies raw materials and food. This sector is as yet little researched and, indeed, is rapidly diminishing in many of the larger cities where land for garden cultivation or fuelwood is being built over.

3   Within the petty-commodity sector there is an exploitative relationship between the entrepreneurs of an enterprise and their labour. Most entrepreneurs own the equipment or the capital necessary for the operation of a business. For example, they own pedicabs which they hire out daily or advance cash for itinerant food hawkers to make purchases at wholesale markets. Exploitation thus occurs within the operations of petty-commodity enterprises.

4   The urban capitalist sector extracts profits from those in petty-commodity enterprises in several ways. In direct terms there is a transfer through the person of the entrepreneur, discussed above, who is frequently, but not always, someone with a waged job. For example, in Indonesia teachers and civil servants are often pedicab owners. Also in direct terms, petty-commodity workers must make payments to the government or its officials in the form of taxes, licence fees, fines (when prosecuted for illegal operations) or bribes (to officials not to prosecute illegal operations). Such payments can slice away a substantial proportion of the actual returns received by workers.

5   Finally, there are the indirect transfers that benefit the urban capitalist sector. These arise because everyone in the city, rich or poor, can purchase goods or services produced by the petty-commodity sector. Their activities thus keep down the cost of living for the already wealthy. At the same time the poor must purchase certain commodities produced by capital enterprises (domestic or foreign), such as kerosene, metal utensils, tools and machinery (for their small businesses); increasingly too, the poor buy imported or prepared food, cigarettes or alcohol with their small surplus income. All of these purchases mean a profit for the manufacturer and constitute an income transfer from poor to rich that far outweighs the smaller returns that flow in the other direction.

Conclusion

It is these wide-ranging benefits which urban capital derives from the petty-commodity activities of the poor that explain why the urban authorities do not use the legislation that already exists to remove such enterprises from the city. Instead what occurs are periodic campaigns to control certain types of activity which may be getting 'out-of-hand' and intruding on the modernization process (squatter settlements are particularly prone to such actions). In short, there exists a 'conservation' process for petty-commodity activities, at least until these activities are either no longer tolerable or else become profitable, when their operations are converted into fully capitalist enterprises. In Malaysia, for example, many of the pedicabs that regularly took children to school have been replaced by minibus services. Such is the fate of those who threaten success within petty-commodity production.

Key ideas

1   Industrialization strategies have been seen as the basis for economic growth in the Third World.
2   Successful development of industry has been confined to only a few countries.
3   Expansion in output does not necessarily generate equivalent growth in employment.
4   Although the informal sector has been a useful concept for appreciating the lifestyle of the poor, it overemphasizes their independence.
5   The petty-commodity approach stresses the exploitative links with capitalist production in the city.

6
Social problems in the city

Introduction

The previous chapters have illustrated the principal forces which have given rise to the enormous social problems facing Third World cities. The rapid population growth has outstripped even the most serious attempts to cope, but too often urban management has ignored the provision of social services and facilities to the poor in favour of economic growth and modernization. The failure of so many urban households to obtain adequate incomes means that they cannot satisfy their own needs to the extent that they would like, so that the informal or petty-commodity sector is left to undertake this provision as best it can, supplemented where expedient by various aided self-help schemes.

In so many cases such programmes are inadequate to meet the real needs of the poor, and serve only to raise social tensions which find an outlet less in urban insurrection (which is usually cleverly controlled by urban managers and their overseas advisers) than in inter-group or intra-household conflict.

The panoply of social pressures, problems and conflicts in the urban Third World is enormous but its manifestation is closely linked to the local circumstances in which global or national forces operate. This chapter must therefore be selective and will cover three different types of social problems in the city, namely, meeting the most basic need, that of low-cost housing; inter-group tensions in ethnically mixed cities; and the changing role of urban women.

The changing economic role of women

Introduction

In the pre-colonial period the status of women in the Third World varied enormously according to local circumstances, with complex mixes of religions, land inheritance and other cultural systems influencing the distribution of economic power and influence. But with the advent of colonialism many of these systems were swept away by the new ownership patterns and labour needs of commercial farming. As the land available to small households dwindled and the demands for cash grew, many men entered into wage labour – usually in rural areas but later in the new colonial cities.

The women who remained on the family or communal land became the main providers for the household since the colonial labour system left little surplus for remittance back to the family. Women therefore assumed even greater labour burdens on communal land and family gardens, marketing any subsistence surplus, engaging in traditional craftwork (such as basket weaving) and, if necessary or possible, undertaking part-time paid employment. All this was in addition to domestic work.

In the post-colonial period, however, this situation changed once more as capitalist values and goods began to penetrate the countryside. Changing urban diets, for example, reduced the demand for surplus local crops, whilst traditional craft products were superseded by cheaper and more sophisticated manufactured commodities. As rural population pressure rose, so women too began to migrate to the cities in search of work, but most remained behind – confined more than ever to a domestic role. The concern of these poor rural women is often not with their own status compared with that of men but with their poverty. What they want is access to better nutrition, health or education. In short, they tend to see themselves as peasants first and women second; the focus of their interests is development and change from a class rather than a gender perspective.

The movement of women to cities presupposes an economic role for them, but the exact nature of this role varies according to social, economic and political factors as well as to the personal qualities of the migrants themselves. We will examine this role through the medium of the most commonly identified areas of employment – the formal, informal (petty-commodity) and domestic sectors.

Formal sector

Several interrelated models have been put forward to explain how the urban wage labour market functions in relation to women. One theory suggests that women are paid less than men because they are less productive, the result of their being less physically strong, prone to greater absenteeism or

Plate 6.1   Harare, Zimbabwe: women waiting for factory work

turnover, and less skilled. Of course, these factors are themselves the consequence of other demands placed on women by their family, together with more limited education and training. Other observers have suggested that as a result of these alleged employment limitations women are confined to particular occupations within which they compete amongst themselves for relatively few positions, thus keeping down wages (plate 6.1).

Despite these apparent discouragements, female labour force participation (FLFP) rates have steadily increased as urban growth has accelerated in the Third World. However, it is true that, in general, in the highly fragmented labour markets female workers tend to be placed in specific lower-paid occupations. These trends in FLFP rates are particularly visible in South-east and East Asia (table 6.1) where they equal and occasionally exceed those in western countries. As a result the female proportion of the urban work force has steadily increased.

The reasons for this increase not only relate to the accelerated demand for the unskilled, short-term, non-unionized and therefore cheap female labour in the factories of the multinational corporations, but also to the general erosion of traditional rural values relating to parental control. It is often difficult to distinguish between these influences in attracting young girls into the city.

Table 6.1 South-east Asia: changing economic participation by gender

	Female labour force participation rate		Female % of total urban employment		Relative growth of male–female employment in the 1970s					
					Manufacturing		Trade		Services	
	1970	1980	1970	1980	Male-female growth ratio	% female employment in sector	Male/female growth ratio	% female employment in sector	Male-female growth ratio	% female employment in sector
South Korea	26.3	30.4	25.3	31.1	1.0	40.8	1.3	34.4	1.2	16.6
Taiwan	26.7	34.2	17.1	32.0	1.6	48.1	2.9	19.9	5.3	27.3
Hong Kong	42.8	49.5	33.7	35.5	1.4	54.1	1.5	22.4	2.4	18.1
Singapore	29.5	44.2	23.6	34.4	1.9	40.8	5.0	21.4	1.7	30.9
Malaysia	28.2	45.0	26.2	–	1.5	35.4	2.0	20.6	2.9	39.1
Thailand	45.1	54.4	39.2	43.4	1.2	23.9	1.3	37.7	1.9	34.0
Philippines	33.7	–	37.4	–	–	23.6	0.2	22.3	0.4	50.2
Indonesia	25.5	27.7	26.4	28.8	1.0	24.1	1.4	41.1	1.4	32.2

Source: Constructed from data in G. Jones (1983) 'Economic growth and changing female employment structure in the cities of South-east and East Asia', unpublished paper, Department of Demography, Australian National University.

Women factory workers in Fiji*

Kusum began work in Suva fifteen years ago when her husband, a carpenter, became unemployed. Although it was against family tradition she started work as a housegirl but, when her employer found a cheaper girl recently arrived from a village, she was dismissed.

Kusum then found work in a series of government factories as a machinist, starting as a trainee at F$7 (£4.70) per week and after thirteen years her wages had risen to F$25 (£16.70) per week. Two years ago she moved to her present job which, although it pays F$30 (£20), has much worse working conditions.

She gets up at 4 a.m. to prepare breakfast for her children and husband, still unemployed, and to do various household chores before leaving for work at 7 a.m. Although the factory does not begin until 8 a.m., workers are expected to make an 'unofficial' start 30 minutes earlier. Once everyone is inside the factory, an iron grill is locked so that no one can go out.

There are about sixty women working under the direct supervision of the owner who insists on intensive work to meet production 'targets' far higher than are possible. No one is allowed to visit the toilet during the day except in the 20-minute morning or 30-minute lunch breaks. Work finishes at 5 p.m. and by 5.30 p.m. Kusum is home preparing the evening meal and cleaning the house. In retrospect, sometimes after several weeks, the weekly wage of F$30 is paid.

Kusum considers her factory to be better than many others where wages average F$15 per week and there is no morning break. However, even in her workplace it is common practice to dismiss workers shortly before their legal annual paid holiday entitlement and then to rehire them in the new year. Kusum's main hope is that her sacrifices will enable her children to complete their education and obtain good jobs so that she can leave the factory and return to domestic work.

* This is a resumé of an account that first appeared in the *Sunday Times* (Fiji) on 13 October 1985.

It is also not exclusively into the manufacturing sector that female migrants move, although in some industries, such as electronics in South-east Asia, women of 15 to 25 years account for 80 to 90 per cent of the labour force. As table 6.1 indicates, it is primarily in the Asian NICs that female industrial employment is growing. But it is also clear that important employment opportunities exist in trade, which for women would primarily be as licensed street vendors, and in the service sector. In the latter context this encompasses a wide range of jobs from those in the expanding tourist industry (hotels, restaurants and even prostitution) to more traditional domestic service in the less industrialized countries, such as the Philippines.

Female participation in the formal wage economy therefore tends to be unstable, short-lived and poorly paid. It can in no sense be considered to constitute a step up in the urban socio-economic system. After marriage women often move into the even more unstable condition of petty-commodity production.

The informal sector

The role of women in the informal sector has only recently begun to be explored, partly due to western assumptions that a woman not employed in the wage economy was by definition confined to domestic activities. However, in many Third World countries the 'myth of the male bread-winner' has been challenged by the evident inability of many men to obtain wage employment. In many households, therefore, the steady if small income is furnished by women's activities in the informal sector, occasionally supplemented by remuneration from casual jobs by the men.

Although a wide variety of petty-commodity activities exist, as noted in the previous chapter, it is claimed that women's activities tend to have a domestic context or to be extensions of domestic work. For example, in many of the NICs women undertake 'outwork' at home – that is contract work for factories, such as pressing out plastic shapes from moulds or sticking labels on garments, often in conjunction with their children. Similarly domestic premises may be used for the preparation of food to be hawked around the streets, or for laundry work, or child-minding.

This domestic influence also allegedly extends to non-domestically located activities. For example, women tend to sell fruit and vegetables (linked to garden duties) rather than meats or hardware. Such associations are even extended to activities such as prostitution. In recent years, however, research has shown that men are often quite willing to undertake so-called 'domestic' activities when this is profitable. Indeed there is evidence to show that it is only when profitability wanes that female domination of certain activities occurs (figure 6.1).

Domestic activities

This is still a problematic area of investigation in Third World studies. Basically the contention is that non-remunerative domestic work is all part of the role that capitalism allocates to women. Their role is to reproduce labour and socialize it in the home into its place within the system. However, such arguments must be weighed very carefully in the Third World where traditional cultural values prevent wholesale transfer of western theories.

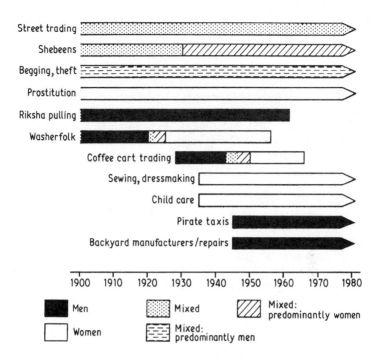

Figure 6.1 Johannesburg: changing male/female dominance of informal sector activities
Source: K. Beavon and C. Rogerson (1986) 'The Changing Role of Woman in the Informal Sector of Johannesburg in D. Drakakis-Smith (ed.) *Urbanization in the Developing World*, London, Croom Helm.

One may also ask why, if this domestic role is so vital to the survival of capitalism, do factories in the Third World city try to attract so many women workers. The response is of course, that such factories utilize female labour before the domestic role begins (after marriage), and it can be extended into informal-sector activities if necessary.

However, perhaps the major problem with the domestic sphere of work in the Third .World is that it also encompasses activities that are non-remunerative but valorizable, i.e. they are of economic value in the context of the household. Such work includes subsistence gardening, the collection of fuelwood, the repair of clothes and similar activities which result in the reduction of family expenditure. These economic roles of women are not uniform to all cities of the Third World. Some activities, such as illegal peri-urban cultivation and fuelwood collection, have almost disappeared in some very crowded cities but may still be important in smaller settlements, particularly in Africa. Much more information is needed on this little appreciated area.

Conclusions

There is a set of standardized responses to the improvement of the status of women within capitalism. It encompasses raising female education levels, establishing work-training programmes, eliminating legal barriers to certain jobs, providing child-care facilities, introducing job flexibility (part-time work) and so on. However, perhaps these have more validity for developed countries than the Third World where women need first to be mobilized on a class rather than a gender basis.

Indeed, in the context of the Third World city we are not yet asking the right questions about women's work and status, let alone finding answers to them. For example, we need to know much more about how women move between the various forms of urban production and reproduction (the domestic, subsistence, informal and formal sectors) during their daily, yearly or life cycle, and to what extent such moves are controlled by dominant class or gender influences or by women themselves. Only when we have more information on these areas can more appropriate policy measures be taken to help improve the status of women.

Ethnicity and urban development: an examination of Malaysia

Malaysia is a small state by Asian standards with under 15 million people, over 80 per cent of whom live in West or Peninsular Malaysia. The remainder live in the Malaysian states of Sarawak and Sabah in North Borneo. The present federation of Malaysian states was formed in 1965, although the Malayan peninsula became independent of Britain in 1957. It is a middle-income country with a good economic growth rate based on primary-commodity exports such as rubber, tin, palm oil, timber and crude oil, although manufacturing exports have clearly grown in recent years (table 6.2).

With just over 30 per cent of the population living in towns and cities, the country is not yet heavily urbanized, but at 5 per cent per annum its urban population is growing rapidly, particularly in Kuala Lumpur, the capital. In ethnic terms just over half the population are Malays, 35 per cent are Chinese and 10 per cent are Indians. At independence the Malays were primarily farmers, the Chinese dominated urban commerce and the Indians were the mainstay of plantation labour. To understand why this ethnic–economic split had occurred, it is necessary to examine the colonial history of the country.

Although the Portuguese took Malacca in 1511 and over the next three hundred years the Dutch and British were involved in mercantile colonialism in the peninsula, there was no real urban impact until the 'industrial' colonial period of the nineteenth century. It was the discovery of tin in

Table 6.2   West Malaysia: selected economic indicators and ethnicity

	Average income (M$)			Gini coefficient*			% labour composition 1981			% labour composition 1980		
	1957	1970	1980	1957	1970	1980	Estates	Mines	Padi	Primary	Secondary	Tertiary
Malays	140	172	513	0.34	0.40	0.47	3	1	97	66	39	47
Chinese	302	381	1094	0.38	0.46	0.58	23	92	1	20	51	42
Indians	243	301	776	0.37	0.47	0.49	74	7	2	13	9	11
All	215	246	763	0.41	0.50	0.57	–	–	–	–	–	–

Note: * The Gini coefficient is a measurement of income distribution. It ranges between 0 (total equality) and 1 (maximum equality).

Sources: M.H. Lim and W. Canat (1981) 'The political economy of state policies in Malaysia', *Journal of Contemporary Asia* 11(1); J.K. Sundaram (1984) 'Malaysia's new economic policy: a class perspective', *Pacific Viewpoint* 25(2).

Malaya that reawakened British interest, although exploitation was actually undertaken by Chinese firms who imported their labour direct from China (6 million between 1880 and 1910). The British intended to stay in their three ports of Penang, Singapore and Malacca (known collectively as the Straits Settlements) controlling exports, until disputes between Malay aristocratic landowners and Chinese mine-owners forced them to move slowly and indirectly into the administration of the Peninsula. It was not until 1909 that the first federation of states occurred. Meanwhile rubber had been introduced and, in order for the Malays to remain as food producers, Indian labour was imported by British plantation managers who had moved over to Malaya.

All this economic development saw the creation for the first time of an urban system, particularly in the wake of railway construction. Almost without exception the towns were dominated by immigrant populations with the British paramount in overseas trade and administration, and the Chinese in all other commercial activities. Thus the Chinese were used as a social and economic buffer between the British and the indigenous Malay peasantry.

The interwar depression brought an end to the primary commodity export boom but by now economic roles were well etablished by race (table 6.2). Many of the established immigrants began to demand better working conditions and equal political rights. The Malays too began to become more political, frustrated they could not make careers in administration or commerce because of their domination by British and Chinese respectively. However, this ostensible ethnic clash had a clear class dimension since it was the wealthy Malays and Chinese who were in conflict over political and economic power. The Chinese proletariat in contrast were attempting to alleviate exploitation by their Chinese employers and socialist trade unions gained ground in the 1930s.

Following the Second World War, the British continued to favour the Malay élite in administration, despite their collaboration with the Japanese. The reason was the Communist insurgency of the 1940s and 1950s which, although anti-colonial in intent, was almost exclusively Chinese in composition. It was countered by British, Malay and Indian military and police units. The outcome of this bitter struggle was the entrenchment of the Malays in political power and the destruction of the Chinese trade-union movement.

In urban terms, although the towns had continued to grow, their institutional morphologies remained dominated by British colonialism, the architecture of which was a hybrid of late imperial grandeur and Muslim elaboration (see plate 2.1). Numerically, however, the cities were still Chinese and their dense shophouse tenements and clan temples were strongly represented too (plate 6.2). At independence in 1957 Singapore, with one million people, was by far the biggest city, with Kuala Lumpur, destined to be the new capital of Malaysia, about one-third as large.

After independence the Malayan government continued to emphasize primary exports and also sought to open new lands in resettlement schemes.

Plate 6.2   Georgetown, Penang: Khoo Kongsi, a traditional clan temple in a district of the city formerly dominated by an extended community

However, many Malay peasants were displaced by the growth of commercial agriculture and moved to the cities where job creation was slow. Despite the optimism, inequality actually increased in Malaysia in the decade following independence (table 6.2) and inter-ethnic tensions built up considerably. The Malay peasants resented their worsening plight and blamed those in the cities (who were mainly Chinese); the poor urban Malays resented Chinese domination of industrial and commercial employment; the Chinese proletariat resented their low wages and blamed the Malaysian government's repression of trade unions; the Chinese bourgeoisie resented their exclusion from government and new industrial development. All of this resentment was ignited by the 1969 elections which resulted in major urban ethnic rioting and several hundred deaths.

Since 1970 economic planning has aimed at eradicating the poverty on which the riots were blamed. But as the poor were mostly rural and therefore Malay, there was an implicit ethnic bias in this objective. Other measures were more explicit in attempting to increase Malay involvement in urban economic development. The major tactic in these changes was an increased role for the state which took the initiative in both investment and control of economic planning. But in order to maintain this position the government has been forced to seek the assistance of foreign business. This increase in state and foreign involvement has been at the expense of domestic Chinese capital, much of which is now invested overseas.

Although these policy changes have caused average Malay incomes to rise, they are still the lowest in absolute terms (table 6.2). Moreover, there is now greater inequality than ever within the groups, which indicates that irrespective of ethnicity, the rich have become richer and the poor have become poorer.

Although Malay migration has had a proportionately greater effect on the smaller east-coast towns, much of the movement has been to Kuala Lumpur. The impact on the capital city has been clear to see with a multinational business centre rising over the old Chinatown and ethnically distinct squatter areas springing up all around the city. In short, what has now appeared in Kuala Lumpur and other Malaysian cities is a complex class and ethnic fragmentation of society whose future is difficult to predict.

Housing for the urban poor

Some definitions

Basically there are three sources of supply for low-cost housing in Third World cities. These may be labelled the public, private and popular sectors (figure 6.2). Of these the public and private sources fall loosely into what we have previously described as the formal sector, housing which is built according to local building standards by legitimate firms through established land, finance, material and labour markets. In contrast, 'popular' housing is that which is constructed by the poor themselves usually in contravention of some legislation, outside established building conventions and below 'acceptable' standards or norms.

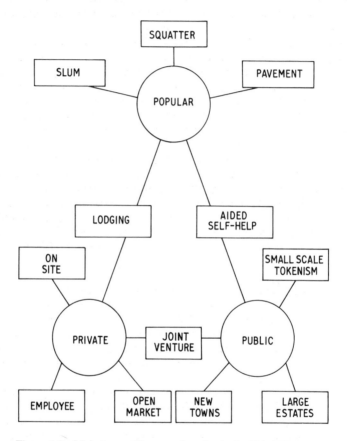

Figure 6.2   Main types of low-cost housing in the Third World

It would be wrong to claim that all low-cost urban housing in the Third World can be neatly placed into one of these three categories. As with the economic activities of the formal and informal sector, housing types vary enormously and often possess characteristics of more than one sector. For example, some of the apartment blocks constructed in Ankara (see case study H) appear to be conventional buildings but have no official occupation permit because they have not been approved or even inspected by the local authority. On the other hand, many dilapidated houses on the edges of rapidly growing cities are perfectly legal dwellings in what were formerly separate villages now surrounded by urban sprawl. Some are abandoned by their owners or tenants, others are held by speculators waiting for land values to rise.

Despite these problems, the basic differences between conventional (formal) and non-conventional housing are still useful in helping to understand the processes by which the state and private enterprise on the one hand, and the poor, on the other hand, respond to the ever growing demand for shelter. Of these sources of housing, the private sector seems obviously to be the least important in meeting low-cost housing needs and this section will not discuss it at great length. However, it is worthwhile to note in passing that it is private-sector firms which actually construct most government housing (on contract), that a hugely inflated demand at times of crises (refugee influxes) provide massive profit opportunities, and that many squatter huts are also built by petty-commodity firms (not by the resident) – so that private-sector involvement is not as limited as might first appear. Moreover, several governments in South-east Asia have experimented with joint-venture schemes to try to meet the housing needs of the 'rising poor', but without subsidy of land costs these have faced serious difficulties.

Popular housing: the response of the poor

There are two different types of popular response by the poor to their shelter needs – squatter housing and slum formation. The former usually comprises structures that are erected illegally, in contravention of building codes and/or on land without the permission of the owner. Slums, in contrast, are permanent buildings that have become substandard through a combination of age, neglect and subdivision (resulting in considerable pressure on basic amenities).

Much of the literature and the official data on urban housing in the Third World fails to distinguish between these two types despite their fundamental differences. Admittedly, in some cities the two blend together in space and form. For example, slum landlords permit squatters to build on roofs (plate I.1) or in yards; or squatters permit others to rent portions of the land or dwelling they occupy. However, to ignore the basic differences is to disregard the dimensions of the housing problem and to underestimate the varied responses needed for it.

Much of the official data on housing needs (usually relating to 'slums' but meaning 'squatter housing') represents a huge underestimate of real needs because it ignores the large numbers housed in dilapidated, overcrowded but permanent housing in older parts of the city. It is my experience,

Plate 6.3   Capetown, South Africa: crossroads squatter camp with Table Mountain in the background

however, that slums are as important as squatter settlements in meeting the needs of the poor. Indeed, it is often claimed that it is in the centrally located slums that migrants first settle in order to be near sources of employment. Later, when other family members appear, there is an incentive to move to the 'more spacious' areas of peripheral squatter settlements (see case study H, following).

Case study H

The *gecekondu* of Ankara, Turkey

Turkey currently has a population of 47 million of which 45 per cent are urbanized. In the immediate post-war decades the Turkish government encouraged many potential migrants to move to Western Europe. Now this has been curtailed by German immigration laws and much of the rural population movement is focused on Turkey's own main cities (figure H.1).

The fastest growing city is the capital, Ankara, which was a small provincial town until 1923 when it was chosen as the capital of the new republic. Since then it has grown from 25,000 to 2.5 million, consistently

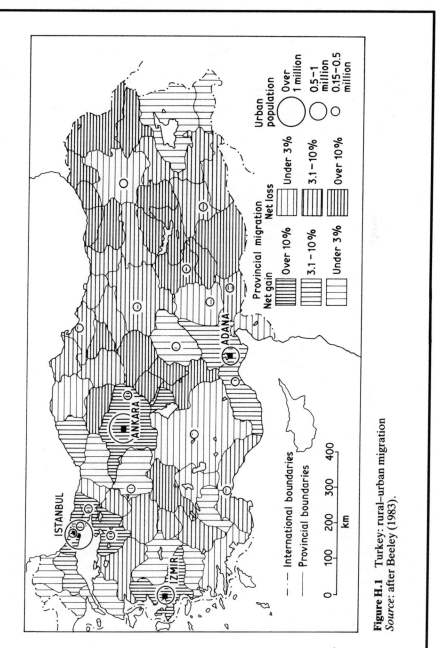

Figure H.1 Turkey: rural–urban migration
Source: after Beeley (1983).

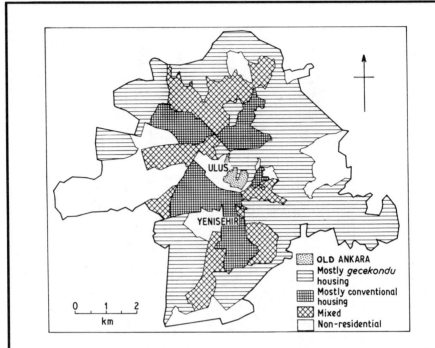

Figure H.2 Ankara: housing types

outstripping the predicted growth of a series of urban plans that have proved incapable of meeting the physical demands of such a population explosion. As a result most migrants have taken matters into their own hands and have built their housing on any available land. The Turkish word for a squatter hut is *gecekondu* which literally translates as 'night-built' and conveys the clandestine nature of the early constructions. Two-thirds of the capital's population is said to live in *gecekondu* housing but many have been granted partial *de facto* or *de jure* rights over the years as politicians have sought favour and votes with such a large section of the community. Despite periodic attempts to prohibit further settlement or to initiate new housing programmes, *gecekondu* construction continues apace but important differences have emerged between the various squatter communities that now dominate the map of Ankara (figure H.2). Particularly marked is the contrast between the older, inner *gecekondu* communities and the newer, peripheral settlements.

Plate H.1   Ankara: older inner-city *gecekondu* (squatter) settlement on steep sided hills near the central business district

One of the older districts in central Ankara is Altindağ, which ironically means 'golden hill', a steep-sided area to the north of the citadel which contains more than 50,000 people, over two-thirds of whom live in wooden *gecekondu* units (plate H.1). Living conditions within the area are very crowded in terms of both ground and housing densities, whilst the majority of households lack adequate water supply, toilet, cooking and washing facilities. Although there is a sizeable minority of more recent arrivals, most of the families are long-term residents of Ankara, more than half having lived in Altindağ itself since the mid 1960s. The low rents in the area and the proximity to job opportunities in the city centre were the main attractions for the residents. This is borne out by the occupational structure which emphasizes employment in petty commerce or service activities, such as street trading.

Very different conditions are found in the extensive peripheral squatter areas. Much of the accommodation here is solidly constructed from stone or brick and is much more spacious, internally and environmentally, than

Case study H (*continued*)

Plate H.2 Anakara: good quality *gecekondu* (squatter) housing on the edge of the city

housing in Altindağ (plate H.2). In addition, the great majority of these units are self-contained with regard to washing, toilet and cooking facilities. The deficiencies in the outer districts are mainly infrastructural, a consequence of their relative newness and distance from the city proper. A large number of houses therefore have no electricity, sewerage or water connections and arrangements for rubbish disposal are poor. Despite these defects such areas are popular with new migrants. Almost half of the residents have lived in Ankara for less than ten years, most coming directly from villages located outside Ankara province. In contrast, the older migrants of Altindağ were more likely to have come from the towns nearer Ankara. Although many outer *gecekondu* districts have only recently been settled, their occupational structures differ markedly from those usually assumed to exist in such areas. Many of the households' heads are in regular, full-time employment in either factories or offices. Some of these jobs involve considerable travel and a sizeable proportion of the workers face journeys to work of at least two hours each day.

Ankara clearly contains two very different types of *gecekondu* settlement, a feature recognized by the residents themselves. A large number of the households in the outer districts formerly lived in the central areas and had moved out in order to obtain better accommodation. The socio-economic contrasts between the inner and outer *gecekondu* areas are such as to pose many problems for a government attempting to deal positively with such settlements. If the disorderly sprawl of Ankara is to be curbed, it is evident that the benign indifference which has existed to date in lieu of effective policies must cease. On the other hand, the *laissez-faire* policies seem to have enabled diligent families to create for themselves a reasonably satisfactory living environment, in spite of problems of confused tenure and deficient infrastructure. But the minimal pre-election improvement manoeuvres which were used to win votes have been recognized for their true worth by a new generation of *gecekondu* residents who are beginning to realize how little the city has given their families over the last two decades. The very names of some of the *gecekondu* districts reflect this new determination – Yiğitler (the courageous), Çaliskanlar (the hardworking) and Yilmazlar (the undaunted).

Squatter settlements are known by a variety of local names – *favalas* in Brazil, *gecekondu* in Turkey, *bidonvilles* in parts of North Africa. In the English language this has spawned a sequence of largely inadequate terms designed to capture the nature of such shelter. Some examples are 'temporary', 'uncontrolled' and 'spontaneous'. But many squatter settlements have been in existence for a long time and their growth has been carefully supervised both by their inhabitants and by the local authorities who can use the illegal nature of the housing or the activities of the residents to demolish and evict whenever they wish.

For many years the residents of slums or squatter settlements were assumed to be the 'flotsam and jetsam' of urban society – poor, mostly migrant households who contributed nothing to the urban economy but increased pressure on the provision of services. According to Oscar Lewis such people lived in a 'culture of poverty' and lacked the ability, incentive or vision to raise themselves from their position. In short, they had not been fully absorbed into the modern, urban way of life and existed on its margins.

Such notions of marginality fitted in particularly well with the peripheral location of many squatter settlements, situated as they were on the edges of the city or on awkward sites too costly to develop commercially. However, as research investigations of poor communities began to proliferate in the 1970s, it became increasingly clear that the poor were not socially, economically and politically marginal to life in the city. Indeed, their vitality and activities were revealed to make essential and important contributions to the urban economy, albeit (as the previous chapter has shown) in an exploited manner. As Janice Perlman has succinctly summarized the situation in her book on the *Myths of Marginality*, the poor are 'not economically marginal but exploited, not socially marginal but rejected, not culturally marginal but stigmatised and not politically marginal but manipulated and repressed'.

What such comments mean is that it is not possible to understand the nature of squatter or slum settlements on the basis of their appearance. Slums, in particular, because of their central location tend to be characterized by very close economic ties with the central business districts and frequently house many family businesses. In consequence, there is often a very wide range of household types and incomes in most slum districts (see case study I, below).

Case study I

A Hong Kong tenement district

Plate I.1   Yau Ma Tei: old tenements with rooftop squatters

Yau Ma Tei, located on the western side of the Kowloon peninsula, was first developed in the 1860s but it was not until the inter-war years between 1920 and 1940 that refugee movement from an unstable China to an increasingly prosperous Hong Kong saw the intense development of three- to four-storey tenements that still characterize much of the area today (plate I.1). A further refugee influx in the late 1940s, together with a deliberate relaxation of building regulations, resulted in massive redevelopment to very high densities.

Peak overcrowding was reached in 1961 when densities averaged more than 1100 per hectare but, despite a fall in the overall population of the district, by the late 1970s there were still 1.8 families for every dwelling unit; most of these were one or two person households (figure I.1). For the most part the accommodation was in tiny tenement rooms set in a congested and dirty environment.

In view of the congestion it is surprising to discover that more than half of the land area comprises road space. But because of the residential densities much of this is used for outdoor living and petty trading activities (figure I.2). In the 1970s some 2800 daytime hawkers operated in the district.

Despite these substandard living conditions rents are relatively high because of the central location adjacent to the tourist central business district of downtown Kowloon. As a result most of the recent redevelopment has been taken up by middle-income owner-occupiers anxious to avoid the rent inflation of the last decade.

Yau Ma Tei thus has a fairly broad income profile and its average income is only slightly lower than that of the colony as a whole. In the late 1970s more than a quarter of the population earned well over the upper limit of eligibility for government housing. Moreover, most of the residents earn their incomes from the myriad of small commercial or industrial enterprises within the district itself which is also an employment focus for many other residents of the Kowloon peninsula. Its vibrant economic life is reflected, too, in the strength of its traditional community organizations that depend for patronage on local businessmen.

In short, Yau Ma Tei is not compatible with the inner-city slums of the west. But its very vitality has also spurred contrasting attitudes from urban planners. Whereas in the west the inner city has increasingly become a focus for government subsidies, districts such as Yau Ma Tei are left to fend for themselves. In the short term this may mean a continuation of petty-commodity input to the urban economy as a whole but in the long term it does little to alleviate the miserable living conditions of the majority of the residents.

Case study I (*continued*)

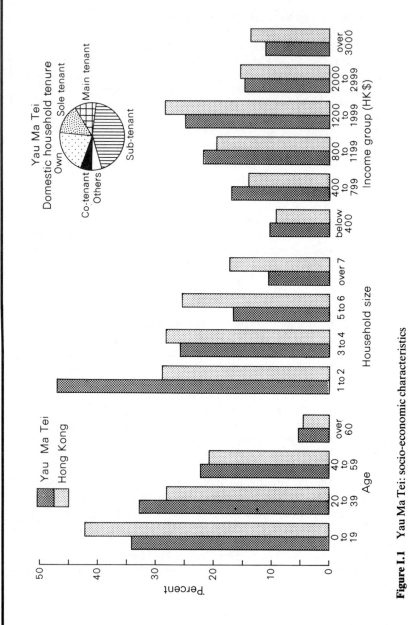

Figure I.1   Yau Ma Tei: socio-economic characteristics

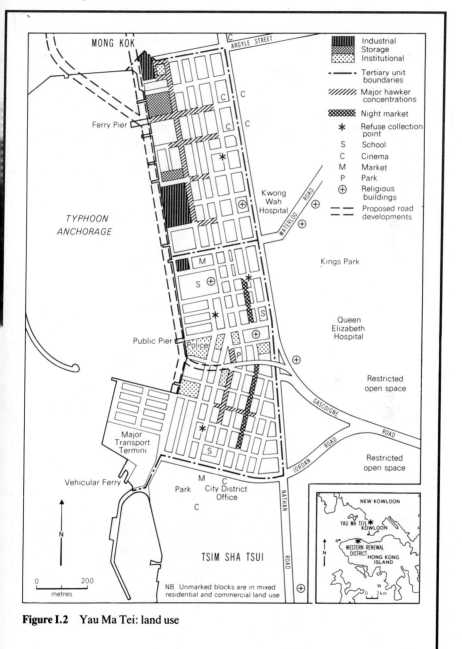

Figure I.2   Yau Ma Tei: land use

Squatter settlements too tend to contain a broader spectrum of activities and individuals than might be expected. Indeed, as John Turner showed more than ten years ago by his studies in Latin America, squatter communities are not only highly organized but also contain a normal range of changing family ambitions and priorities. Turner claimed that because they are poor, however, such households are forced to choose between these priorities; the consequent balance of job proximity, cheap rents and access to various amenities (such as education or retail facilities) governs the type and location of their accommodation.

John Turner developed a simple model to show how these conflicting priorities change as low-income households become more securely established in the urban economy (figure 6.3). At the earliest 'bridgeheader' stage access to casual work is the most important consideration and any nearby

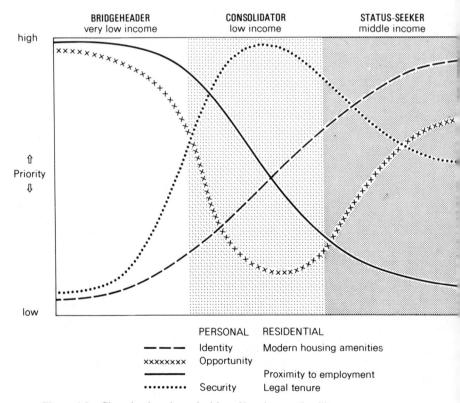

Figure 6.3   Changing housing priorities of low-income families

shelter will suffice; later when a more regular and reliable income has been obtained the main objective is to 'consolidate' one's position in the city by means of securing legal tenure; finally, once legal residence has been secured, priorities are given to enhancing the lifestyle of the family by improving access to other amenities. Turner claimed that upwardly mobile families would either move to accommodation that satisfied these changing needs or stay in a community that was itself being upgraded.

The value of Turner's work was that, almost for the first time, squatters were seen as normal residents of the city in terms of their needs, their ambitions and their determination to achieve these. As a result, squatter settlements began to be looked upon much more positively by policy-makers (at least by those in the international agencies who controlled the aid programmes) as normal, even healthy, manifestations of urban growth in the Third World. As such, advisers claimed, squatters should not be condemmed and evicted; instead their energies should be used and channelled into government-assisted improvement programmes. This assumption has formed the basis of many housing schemes over the past ten years.

However the situation is neither so encouraging nor optimistic for the poor. For one thing, the growth of circular migration, noted in chapter 3, has meant that many urban residents are no longer as committed to improving their living conditions along the lines that Turner suggested. However, the main criticism has come from radical observers who have claimed that squatters, like all urban poor, do not have full freedom of choice to pursue their various priorities with regard to housing. Instead, such critics argue, their poverty and the domination of urban managers (as discussed in chapter 4) severely restrict the options open to them. Consequently it is morally wrong to regard squatter or slum settlements as 'normal' manifestations of urban growth. In reality, such housing is a reflection of unequal access to urban resources and aided self-help programmes merely perpetuate these inequalities.

But here the discussion is overlapping into the realms of government housing programmes and to fully appreciate this criticism we must review the whole spectrum of such responses.

Public housing: the response of the state

Government responses to low-income housing needs are dictated by many considerations, of which perhaps the least important is the welfare of poor. In analysing these responses it is important to remember that there is a basic distinction to be made between policies *towards* housing – the macropolicies that determine the overall level of investment – and policies *for* housing – the ways in which the investment is actually spent.

Macropolicies are influenced by all of the processes that have shaped development in general in the Third World, from the basic political philosophy of the state, to strategies on modernization and westernization, to attitudes towards the role of the city in the development process and, most important, to views on the relative importance of social and economic objectives. In so many Third World countries the welfare of the poor is seen as an unappealing social overhead that consumes investment without creating growth. Even when a commitment to social programmes is present, housing must compete against education, health care and other basic needs for limited funds.

It is only in recent years that more convincing (in the eyes of most development planners) arguments have emerged to influence investment in low-cost housing for the urban poor. Some of these arguments relate to economic productivity and relate to the asssumption that a better-housed work-force will be healthier and more productive. Others are linked to growing fears that the proliferation of a discontented, underprivileged poor will bring about urban political instability and threaten multinational profits (see chapter 4). In some locations, both of these sets of arguments have fused together and encouraged massive housing programmes – as in Singapore or Hong Kong (see case study I). Even within such large-scale housing commitments, therefore, one would have to look very closely to discern a strong welfare motivation. In most Third World countries even the political and economic arguments for low-cost housing investment cut little ice with urban managers until the advent of aided self-help schemes which appealed because of their low-cost, low commitment to social reform and high aid content.

But few governments are committed to any consistent policy at all, beyond total disregard, and the use made of investment funds (from domestic or external sources) varies enormously. The following list comprises only the simplest of illustrative categorizations:

1   The most common response to the proliferation of popular housing is that of eradication in order to 'get rid' of troublesome squatters and improve the image of the city. Demolition and eviction schemes are, however, seldom successful even when accompanied by various measures to try to prevent migration to the city (see chapter 2). Eventually those who want to return to the city do so, despite the risks.

2   Other authorities make token responses to the housing needs of the poor, usually in the form of a relatively limited but highly visible project designed more to impress electorates or visitors than to meet real low-cost housing needs.

3   The principal problem with these and more extensive conventional schemes is usually that they are very costly and therefore beyond the financial capability of the poor. The root cause is the imported, western technology on which urban planners have depended for their housing

programmes. Unsuitable designs that require imported materials and even labour are all too common in Third World cities and prove even more unpopular when located on the urban periphery, far away from jobs, because of land costs. It is little wonder that so much of the allegedly low-cost housing constructed in this way eventually ends up as middle-income accommodation because of the inability of the poor to meet rental levels.

4 In a few countries, public housing provision has escalated to the level of 'new towns' but these are seldom self-contained economic and social units and function primarily as industrial estates/middle-class suburbs. Petaling Jaya, for example, is only 10 km outside Kuala Lumpur and the principal road linking the two is thronged with reverse commuting all day, with middle-income Petaling Jaya inhabitants travelling to and from white-collar employment in the capital, and blue-collar factory workers from the low-cost housing areas of Kuala Lumpur streaming to their factory jobs in the 'new town'.

5 Urban renewal, as a form of investment in improved housing, is a rarity in the Third World because so few authorities could contemplate demolishing any of their already limited stock of permanent housing, no matter how dilapidated. Complicated and costly compensation problems are also a discouragement. Only where very strong motivation exists have governments become involved in such schemes, for example in Singapore, where slum clearance provided the double bonus of fragmenting the physical heart of radical opposition parties, whilst providing vacant land for the modernization of the central business district. The possibility of rehabilitation of some of the old colonial district seldom seems to merit consideration.

Case study J

Government housing programmes in Hong Kong

Hong Kong is a colony of some 5.6 million people which has been administered by Britain since 1842 and is scheduled to be returned to China in 1997. For the last thirty years it has had a public housing programme second to none in its extent which now houses almost two-thirds of the colony's population. But welfare motives have played only secondary roles in the evolution of this programme, as the following historical review of the three major phases in the programme clearly illustrate.

Case study J (*continued*)

Prior to 1954 the economic disruption of the traditional entrepôt functions of the colony by the wars in China and Korea discouraged the government from accommodating the massive refugee population, apart from extending a benign indifference towards both the illegal dwellings which sprang up around the colony and the intensive subdivision of existing tenements. But by 1954 the government's hand had been forced by a massive fire in Shek Kip Mei, Kowloon, which made more than 50,000 squatters homeless. Following this incident it was decided to embark on a large-scale programme of high-rise resettlement housing. The initial standards were undoubtedly low and the government admitted that the density, ventilation and amenities of the new blocks were not satisfactory,

Plate J.1   Hong Kong: early public housing with communal facilities and few estate amenities

although it was hoped that the design would permit later improvements along these lines. Given the economic uncertainties of the time this approach was perhaps understandable; its retention for a further ten years, whilst the colony prospered, is more difficult to justify (plate J.1).

In fact, the adherence to these minimum standards reflected the priorities of the government towards its resettlement programme. The overriding objective was to acquire valuable building land for redevelopment rather than resettle squatter families on welfare grounds. Not until much later did the Housing Board recommend that consideration should be given to resettlement of squatters living in the worst housing conditions, in addition to people from areas cleared for redevelopment, or to the poorest tenement dwellers. As a result, between 1954 and 1964 the number of squatters in the colony increased by 350,000, in spite of the resettlement programme. Some of the new squatters were immigrants; some had voluntarily moved out of their legal accommodation to take advantage of inflated rents; but most had been displaced from the old central tenements by private redevelopment schemes.

The second phase of housing development in Hong Kong began in 1964 when the government reassessed the situation and decided that its housing programme was too limited, and needed to be extended and upgraded. One of the major problems which affected all public housing during this second phase was the increasing tendency for new estates to be located on the urban periphery, some distance from the main employment centres (figure J.1). For a time this resulted in long delays in filling the estates, but steady improvement in both employment opportunities and transport have eased the difficulties. The problems encountered in developing these peripheral districts encouraged a change in policy in favour of the two new towns of Tsuen Wan and Kwun Tong which received substantial investment in both residential and industrial construction.

Two features distinguished these early new towns in Hong Kong from their predecessors in Britain. The first was the amount of government low-cost housing which was constructed within the development programme; approximately 70 per cent of the residential units in each of the settlements were built by the government. The second was the proximity of Kwun Tong and Tsuen Wan to the existing metropolitan core. Neither is more than 10 km away from the Kowloon peninsula to which they are connected by dense public and private development.

In terms of quantity there is no doubt that between 1964 and 1973 the

Case study J (*continued*)

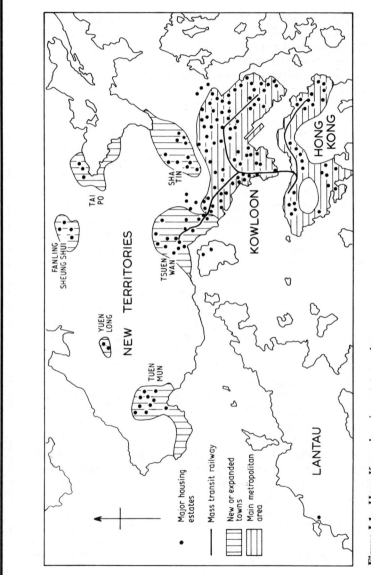

Figure J.1 Hong Kong: housing estates and new towns

Case study J (*continued*)

public housing programme was a great success. The numbers living in all types of government accommodation rose from 0.8 million in 1964 to 2.2 million by 1973, surpassing for the first time the proportion housed in the conventional private sector. But despite this activity the fact remained that in 1973 a great many people lived in the most appalling conditions. Notwithstanding the number of development clearances and the vigorous demolition of new illegal structures, there were still 272,000 squatters, not including the unenumerated people who arrived after 1964. Part of the reason for this was the shift in the building programme to larger sites in peripheral areas where there were fewer squatters to be cleared; but there had also been an attempt to alleviate some of the worst overcrowding in the oldest of the government's own estates. As a result an increasing proportion of new public housing was being taken up by reallocation of existing tenants, rather than accommodating families from slum or squatter districts. Meanwhile the sharp downturn in private-sector construction activity in the late 1960s had also worsened conditions in the central areas so that by 1974 some 750,000 were living in substandard tenements. All together, over 1.4 million were still poorly housed in metropolitan Hong Kong at the end of the second decade of its housing programme.

The current phase of Hong Kong's housing programme began in 1973 when another ten-year housing programme was outlined involving the rehousing of some 2 million people by 1983. Many of the new objectives were a consequence of the first and most important change which was initiated, namely the amalgamation of all housing agencies and departments into one co-ordinated Housing Authority responsible for planning, clearance, construction and management of all public housing.

The main features of government housing programmes since 1974 can be divided into two broad groups. First, there are the principal supply characteristics: the emphasis on new-town and New Territory developments; the continued improvement programme in the old estates; the improvements in flat and estate design; and the recent introduction of a home-ownership scheme within existing and planned estates: the incursion into commercial development; the revised allocation system; and the general improvement of management and maintenance systems.

One of the most crucial policy changes made by the Housing Authority since 1973 has been to give increased emphasis to comprehensive planning. At the macrolevel this has involved a review of the new-towns programme and its extension to sites much further from the metropolitan core. In 1974 it

Case study J (*continued*)

Plate J.2   Hong Kong: a well-designed and planned new town

was estimated that the existing metropolitan area of Kowloon, New Kowloon and Hong Kong Island could accommodate only another 250,000 people in new government housing. This meant that most of the ten-year target would have to be housed in the New Territories, and to this end six new towns have been planned with a combined intended population of some 3 million, two-thirds of whom will live in government housing. At present, the programme is well on target with the comprehensively planned towns appealing to both private developer and prospective resident alike. Already the population growth of the main metropolitan area has appreciably slowed, whilst that of Sha Tin and Tuen Mun, in particular, surges ahead (plate J.2).

A second, important change in policy relates to the belated introduction of housing aimed specifically at the middle-income groups. For many years

Case study J (*continued*)

such families had been ineligible for government housing and yet were unable to afford adequate accommodation on the spiralling private market. In 1978 a modest home-ownership scheme was introduced by a still sceptical Housing Authority but the enthusiastic response soon led to an expansion up-market.

In general terms, since 1954 the Hong Kong government has built accommodation for almost two-thirds of the population. Not only are the dimensions of the programme impressive but it would also be true to say that most of the units are low cost. However, as recent analysis of current trends in the construction and allocation of government housing has shown, access to such units is becoming increasingly biased in both social and spatial terms. This has become particularly noticeable with the success of new-town developments in the New Territories and the middle-income housing programmes. The consequence of both these successes has been a diminution of interest in and development of the older, blue-collar districts in the metropolitan areas. Nowhere is this more evident than in the fate of the Western District urban renewal scheme which was selected for comprehensive redevelopment in 1965 but which has degenerated into slum clearance for the benefit of private, commercial schemes.

It must not be deduced from these critical comments that there are no praiseworthy features to government housing policies in Hong Kong; given the dimension of the programme it would be surprising if many families had not received substantial benefits. Nevertheless, such benefits have been secondary to the economic and political objectives which have undoubtedly given impetus to government investment in housing at the level of national development policy.

Aided self-help: the acceptable face of capitalism?

Aided self-help programmes, as noted earlier in this section, are based on a combination of public and popular action. The government assists, in areas such as materials, funds or training, low-income households to improve their living environments. There are various kinds of aided self-help housing programmes currently in operation. The simplest is that of upgrading squatter settlements – putting in essential infrastructure such as sewerage or water reticulation. As these schemes leave most squatters *in situ*, they are popular with the residents. But infrastructural redevelopment of existing sites is very expensive, much more so than upgrading the dwelling itself through the provision of subsidized materials. It is the latter which thus tends to be more favoured. Moreover, most governments are reluctant to grant parallel tenure rights to those living in valuable central locations.

The second major type of programme is the site and service scheme. Prepared lots with minimum services, usually water, sewerage and electricity, are made available in designated areas. A more sophisticated and expensive version is where a small core-house is also provided. In both cases, the residents are encouraged to self-build (or contract out) the eventual family home. The principal attraction of such schemes is the accompanying tenure; the major problems are unpopular peripheral locations (this is usually where large tracts of vacant land exist) and the stringency of rental demands and construction completion dates. Once again, there is considerable evidence that successful construction, as in plate 6.4, tends to be linked to 'invading' middle-income households or to those who sublet part of the eventual house in order to make ends meet and thereby re-create conditions of overcrowding.

Plate 6.4   Harare, Zimbabwe: piecemeal improvement of a core house by an upwardly mobile family

But the principal criticism must be, as with so many other attempts to 'help' the urban poor, that they are involved only as a source of cheap labour and take almost no part in the overall planning and decision-making process. At the end of the day even those who are residing in improved accommodation have not changed their relative position within the city. They are still poor and still live in ghettoes of underprivilege.

This brings us to a convenient but apposite conclusion for the whole of this chapter because improvements in accommodation, or health care or education cannot be seen as ends in themselves. They are part of a seamless web of basic needs for the poor, all of which focus on the central thread of income and employment. Real improvement in any one of these basic needs is heavily dependent on improving the access of the poor to employment with fair and adequate recompense. Not to recognize this basic fact is to condemn many Third World cities to an unstable and uncertain future.

Key ideas

1   Women and the city
    (a) In general the status of women does not reflect their economic contribution to household and urban economies.
    (b) The economic role of women shifts between various sectors of the urban economy.
2   Ethnicity and the city
    (a) In many cities ethnic factors are as important as class factors in economic imbalance.
    (b) Many of the ethnic problems result from colonialism.
3   Housing in the city
    (a) Many of the poor meet their own housing needs.
    (b) Slums are as important as squatter settlements in housing the poor.
    (c) The response of the state has been limited and tends to provide expensive and unsuitable western-style housing.
    (d) Those cities with extensive programmes have not responded purely from welfare motives.

Further reading and review questions

Chapter 1

1   Use figure 1.1 to compare the levels of urban population in the developed and developing countries. Account for the major differences.
2   Compare the rates of urban growth between countries within the Third World. How do these relate to economic indicators?
3   What is urban primacy and what relevance does it have for the study of urbanization in the developing world?

Further reading

Drakakis-Smith, D. (1981) *Urbanization, Housing and the Development Process*, London, Croom Helm.
Gilbert, A. and Gugler, J (1982) *Cities, Poverty and Development*, Oxford, Oxford University Press.
King, A. (1976) *Colonial Urban Development*, London, Routledge & Kegan Paul.

Chapter 2

1   What were the main features of mercantile colonialism and how did they affect colonial settlement?
2   What were the major forces transforming economic objectives into urban form in the nineteenth century? Illustrate your answer with reference to a case study.

3   What were the major contrasts between urban growth in the late colonial and early independence periods?
4   In what ways has the evolution of the New International Division of Labour affected contemporary cities in the Third World?

Further reading

McGee, T.G. (1967) *Southeast Asian City*, London, Bell.
King, A. (1976) *Colonial Urban Development*, London, Routledge & Kegan Paul.
Goodfriend, D. (1982) 'Shahjahanabad – Old Delhi: tradition and planned change', *Ekistics* 49(297).

Chapter 3

1   Assess the relative importance of the migrational and natural components of urban growth in the Third World.
2   What are the major characteristics of contemporary rural to urban migration?
3   Why do some cities have high rates of natural growth and what should be done about this?

Further reading

World Bank (1986) *World Development Report 1985*, Washington DC.
Pryor, R. (1981) *Migration and Development in Southeast Asia*, Oxford, Oxford University Press.
Drakakis-Smith, D. (1976) 'Slums and squatters in Ankara', *Town Planning Review* 47(3).
Jones, G.W. and Richter, H.V. (eds) (1981) *Population Mobility and Development: Southeast Asia and the Pacific*, Monograph 27, Canberra, Development Studies Centre, Australian National University.

Chapter 4

1   Why have many national governments taken control of capital-city management?
2   What form has this management taken?
3   Why have the urban poor not reacted more violently to continued deprivation?
4   What political actions do the urban poor take in the Third World?

Further reading

Ward, P. (1981) 'Political pressure for urban services', *Development and Change* 12.

Drakakis-Smith, D. and Rimmer, P. (1982) 'Taming the wild city: urban management in Southeast Asia's capital cities', *Asian Geographer* 1(1).
Bello, W., Kinley, D. and Elinson, E. (1982) *Development Debacle: the World Bank in the Philippines*, Birmingham, IFDP, Third World Publications.

Chapter 5

1 Is it realistic for developing countries to seek to achieve economic development by means of an industrial revolution as happened in the west?
2 Has industrial growth created sufficient jobs to absorb urban migrants?
3 What is the informal sector? Give examples of such activities in the sectors of housing, transport, manufacturing, and services.
4 Does the informal sector provide a self-contained way of life for the urban poor?

Further reading

Bromley, R. (1979) *The Urban Informal Sector*, London, Pergamon.
Rimmer, P., Drakakis-Smith, D. and McGee, T.G. (1978) *Challenging Unconventional Wisdom: Food, Shelter and Transport in Southeast Asia and the Pacific*, Monograph HG12, Canberra, Australian National University.
Rogerson, C. (1985) 'The first decade of informal sector studies', *Environmental Studies* 25.

Chapter 6

1 What are the different sectors of the urban economy to which women contribute?
2 Why have women increasingly been incorporated into factory work in the Third World city in recent years?
3 Apart from Malaysia, what other developing countries exhibit problems of ethnic or cultural conflict and why?
4 What forms does ethnic rivalry take in the Third World city?
5 What are the main ways the poor are housed in the Third World city?
6 Why have governments failed to respond adequately to the housing problems of the poor?
7 Should squatter settlements be demolished as unhealthy or should they be retained and improved?

Further reading

Drakakis-Smith, D. (1979) *High Society: 25 Years of Public Housing in Hong Kong*, Hong Kong, Hong Kong University Press.

Phillips, D. and Yeh, A. (1983) 'Filipinos help themselves to housing', *Geographical Magazine* 65(3).

Murison, H. and Lea, J.P. (1979) *Housing in Third World Countries*, Sydney, Macmillan.

Momsen, J. and Townsend, J. (1984) *Women's Role in Changing the Face of the Developing World*, Durham, Department of Geography, University of Durham.

Jackson, J. and Rudner, M. (eds) (1979) Issues in Malaysian Development, Singapore, Heinemann.

Clarke, C., Ley, D. and Peach, C. (eds) (1984) *Geography and Ethnic Pluralism*, London, Allen & Unwin.

Index